SPEAKING THE TRUTH IN LOVE

LESSONS I'VE LEARNED ABOUT FAMILY COMMUNICATION

BY STEVE DEMME

This book is dedicated to my ever supportive, always faithful, loving wife and my patient, forgiving, teachable sons who learned along with me.

May it encourage those families whose hearts have been turned towards God and towards each other.

"Let the words of my mouth and the meditation of my heart be acceptable in your sight, O LORD, my rock and my redeemer." (Psalms 19:14)

SPEAKING THE TRUTH IN LOVE

LESSONS I'VE LEARNED ABOUT FAMILY COMMUNICATION

INTRODUCTION TO SPEAKING THE TRUTH IN LOVE

Most of what I've learned about communication, I acquired in the past few years. My wife and I began Math-U-See in 1990. This is an education business which uses colorful blocks to teach math. Everyone in our family worked in some aspect of the business for the first several years. We assembled books and shipped them out from our basement. Over the years God prospered our enterprise and it grew and we added employees and purchased a building to house the operation.

The years flew by and our sons attended college and found godly spouses. One at a time they chose to work for the company. By 2011 we were all working for the company with varying levels of involvement. Around this time the thought began to form in my mind, "Why don't we make this a family owned company?" We would all be joint owners, have regular board meetings, and make decisions together.

For over thirty years I have been teaching, preaching, and writing about the importance of the family in the plan of God. I'm totally committed to the concept of family in general and my family in particular. I thought this would be an easy transition, because it aligned with our values as a family. I was never more wrong.

Transitioning from a one-man entrepreneurship

to a family corporation turned out to be one of the hardest things I ever had to do. Entrepreneur sounds noble and cutting edge. In reality it was a dictatorship. The business had become more than a way to provide for my family, it had become my baby and a source of my identity. I have written a book on how God helped me in this difficult season of my life, entitled Crisis to Christ. When we began this process, what was to become the hardest year of my life was still in the future.

Let's go back to the process of transitioning to a family owned corporation. One of the first things we did was to hire a consultant who sat down with us individually to find out what we were thinking. I don't know how much you know about family businesses, but you can make or break a family if you engage in this endeavor. There are benefits and advantages to working with other family members; there is also tremendous potential to wreck a family.

Before the Demmes began meeting as a group to develop our bylaws, articulate a vision statement, and make other necessary decisions, our consultant, Mike, asked us to develop a communication code of conduct. I had never heard of anything like this, and it turned out to be ground rules for how we were to communicate at our family meetings. Some of the ideas were obvious; "listen to each other without interrupting" and "watch your tone." Others rules were very helpful but new to me, such as; "avoid ultimatums" and "try not to take information personally." With Mike's help we came up with a dozen rules of conduct. We even appointed a sheriff to enforce them. Each board meeting of Demme Learning began with prayer and the reading of our code of conduct.

Most of the difficulty in this transition was directly tied to my own issues. As we began learning how to communicate, and with the quiet, steady influence of our consultant Mike, I discovered I was the one who struggled the most with this transition. After several months of painful self-discovery I sought the help of a therapist. I engaged Steve as a therapist, and he was extremely helpful to me as I began to work through my issues. As I got to know more about him, I found out he was a published author in the field of family therapy and taught a class on the same topic. I had learned so much from him and I wanted to learn more. The next fall I bought a backpack and took the train from Lancaster, Pennsylvania to Philadelphia and became a student again at the Council for Relationships.

I drank in each of the lectures, but one of the key takeaways from Steve's course was what I learned about the importance of communication in healthy relationships. During one lecture, Steve encouraged each us to create an outline for teaching the basic principles of communication. He said after years of counseling, one of the primary skills he tries to teach couples is how to talk to one another. I took this assignment seriously, and what you are about to read is the result of my own study, the experience of our family, and the skills I have acquired as my wife and I have learned how to hear each other.

The ability to communicate about difficult decisions around topics like business, values, your occupation, and a family's legacy is essential. Learning and applying these principles transformed our marriage and family. We went through a challenging season for a few years and are now in a much better place. My wife and I have weekly communication times set aside. Wednesday mornings at 10:00 a.m., we convene for what we have termed our weekly "chair chat."

I hope the principles we have learned and applied to such benefit in our own home and business will be a help to you on your journey. May God continue to teach and help us each to speak the truth in love in a way that encourages and builds up the speaker and the listener.

Lord willing, I will be adding study guides and small group materials for this book. Check back here for these resources, www.buildingfaithfamilies.org/speakingthetruth/

Steve

OVERVIEW BY CHAPTER

Chapter 1 reminds us death and life are in the power of the tongue. We have the power to hurt and the opportunity to bless by how we speak.

God's word reminds us our tongue is connected to our heart. **Chapter 2** discusses the importance of the heart and encourages us to have God search our innermost being.

Chapter 3 teaches when the heart is right, the tongue will follow suit. While speaking techniques are valuable, lets begin by asking God to help us have a quiet heart resting in the knowledge God is our Dad and loves us to pieces.

We are encouraged in **Chapter 4** to think well of the person to whom we are speaking. For when we value them as a child of God and created in His image we will be mindful to esteem them highly.

Creating a safe place is essential to nurturing communication. **Chapter 5** articulates the need to understand what is being said without any debate.

Having established a healthy foundation, we begin to discuss specific strategies for the speaker in **Chapter 6**.

Chapter 7 gives several tips on what a good listener can do to really hear what is being communicated.

When the speaker is finished talking the listener has a chance to ask and explore more about what has been said in **Chapter 8**.

Processing what has been learned and walking in each other's shoes are valuable skills which are discussed in more detail in **Chapter 9**.

Everything worth learning and doing can be enhanced by practice. In **Chapter 10** we have questions and suggestions to guide your follow through.

When a couple is becoming proficient they may want to share their new found skills with their family. In **Chapter 11**, several reminders and experiences encourage this process.

When communicating is necessary but not going well, call for help. **Chapter 12** recommends a third party to facilitate safe discussion.

Chapter 13 reminds us loving relationships do not just happen. They are built through verbal and nonverbal communication.

Finally, **Chapter 14** has a list of scripture passages referenced in each of the sections along with additional verses pertaining to communication.

CHAPTER 1:
THE POWER OF
THE TONGUE

As a husband and father I have the potential to build up my family like no one else. I also have the ability to harm my family and wound them. It seems the closer people are and the more love we have for each other, the greater the potential to hurt and be hurt. This is a sobering responsibility. With encouraging words I can build up my wife and sons, and with sharp and harmful words I can discourage and bruise their innermost person.

As Christians, we recognize "death and life are in the power of the tongue." (Proverbs 18:21) "Sticks and stones may break my bones, but words will never hurt me" is not in scripture and is completely inaccurate. We all know we can hurt a person's body by hitting with a stick, but we will wound their spirit with harmful words. On the contrary, scripture reminds us "A gentle tongue is a tree of life, but perverseness in it breaks the spirit." (Proverbs 15:4)

The third chapter of the book of James has a long passage on the power of the tongue. The tongue is compared to a tiny bit in the mouth of a horse, a small rudder guides a large ship, and a little flame can destroy a forest. Words have tremendous potential for good or ill. "With it [our tongue] we bless our Lord and Father, and with it we curse people who are made in the likeness of God. From the same mouth come blessing and cursing. My brothers, these things ought not to be so." (James 3:9–10)

As a speaker, I have often prayed this prayer when I am about to address a roomful of people at a convention. "The Lord God has given me the tongue of those who are taught, that I may know how to sustain with a word him who is weary." (Isaiah 50:4) I regularly look to God for a tongue to sustain weary people and bring them encouragement and refreshment.

I want to have a similar tongue when I talk with those who are most dear to me. During the past few years I have learned the painful truth of how my actions and words have negatively impacted my wife and sons. Thanks to God's gracious intervention in my life, I'm taking steps to restore our relationships, but I had no idea how difficult communication was for our family. The primary reason I was not aware of how my behavior wounded them, is I took personally whatever was said. As you can imagine, this made it very difficult for them to tell me what I needed to hear. My number one desire now is to be kind and thoughtful. I so want my words and actions to not cause harm to those who are nearest and dearest to me.

I am discovering blurting out damaging words and then apologizing does not undo the harm. Words go deep. With just a moment to reflect, I can remember harsh things said to me over fifty years ago. They still hurt me. We can't take back what has been said. There is no amount of repentance or restitution to undo the injury from an unkind word.

With a deepening relationship with God and an increasing awareness of God's love for me, I am seeing positive ways to communicate and hopefully end the cycle of hurt, guilt, and remorse in my relationships. It is my fervent hope If one person reads these words and can pause before saying something he or she will regret, then the writing of this book will have been a success.

As parents, how I use words can have a lifetime effect on my children. If my son does something wrong or makes a bad decision, which we all do, I have to be careful how I address the problem. I could say, "You made a bad call today." Perhaps I will punish him for his actions. This is part of my job as his Dad. But if I say, "You made a bad decision, and you are a loser," then I have crossed the line between correcting his actions and attacking his person. I need to make a distinction between what he did and who he is. As a father, I want to affirm my love for, and commitment to my son, while faithfully admonishing him for the infraction.

I can still remember being told, as a child, "You could wreck a free lunch" or "you could screw up a one car funeral." To this day I don't remember what I did, but I recall those exact words and they still affect me. Yes, I made mistakes, but my actions do not make me a loser.

Perhaps this is why I still have difficulty believing I am God's adopted son and I am loved and liked for who I am and not based on what I do. I worked so hard for years to do good things because I mistakenly thought this was the path to pleasing God and others. I am finally beginning to experience and believe the unconditional, unchanging affection of my Heavenly Father. God's love doesn't change because God doesn't change. He is God, who changes not. He is the same yesterday, today, and forever.

When I sin or make a mistake, I still have to confess, ask forgiveness, and make restitution when appropriate, but I am still God's son throughout the process. My adoption is not revoked by my behavior. Nothing can separate me from the love of God in Christ Jesus, nothing.

Prayer

Father open my eyes to the impact of my words and anoint my conversations with everyone I meet, especially those who are closest to me. Let my speech be seasoned with salt, and may I have a gentle tongue to bring life and refreshment. In the name of Jesus, Amen.

CHAPTER 2:
THE HEART AND
TONGUE ARE
CONNECTED

Often when you hear a lecture or sermon the importance of good communication in relationships, the speaker will focus on techniques and strategies to help you speak more clearly, improve your listening skills, or help you address difficult topics. And while all of those are helpful, and will even be discussed in this book, it is paramount we understand the foundational role the condition of one's heart in his or her ability to listen and communicate well.

The "heart" in scripture refers to the real person inside of us. When everything is stripped away, the heart is what we value. It reflects our true self. We get a glimpse into the inner workings of our heart of hearts by what we treasure or value. "Where your treasure is, there will your heart be also." (Luke 12:34) What we consider important, treasure, and hold dear, sheds light on the state of our heart.

What we say in an unguarded moment is also a window into our heart. I have heard people blurt out something which they instantly regret. They quickly say, "Oops, I didn't' mean to say that." If I feel comfortable with them, I usually say, "Yes you did. You just didn't mean for me to hear it!" I know this because scripture teaches, "Out of the abundance of the heart the mouth speaks. The good person out of his good treasure brings forth good, and the evil person out of his evil treasure brings forth evil." (Matthew 12:34–35) The heart and the tongue are very much connected.

The heart is vitally important because we believe with our heart, and Jesus dwells in our heart by faith. When the heart is settled, at peace, resting in the Lord, and soft, then we are able to begin learning strategies for how to speak and listen. If the heart is in a state of rebellion, no amount of books or workshops will help the way you communicate.

Recently, my son John, Sandi, and I drove to a wedding held over 200 miles away. We drove there, participated in the pictures and reception, and returned the same day, for a round trip of over 400 miles. Since I do all the interstate driving in our family, my wife and son blissfully slept while I pressed on.

The next morning she awoke happy and perky but I was exhausted. I was weary and bone tired from the journey. When she enthusiastically greeted me in the morning I simply said, "I need some space. I'm not in a good place." She smiled, thanked me for communicating and let me rest.

In the past, I would have pretended to be okay and gamely tried to be nice. She would have quickly discerned something was amiss, then after wondering what she may have done to cause this, withdrawn, and subsequently blamed herself for the distance in our relationship and read another marriage book.

If I were able to muster some energy, I may have approached her and asked her forgiveness for my response. But she would be left still wondering what she did. Unless God granted a miracle, we would have existed this way for days or even weeks before we were able to be close again.

Guess what we do now? We communicate. We try to honestly assess how we are feeling and tell each other. When I awakened in the morning I knew my spirit was fragile because I was emotionally and physically exhausted. When I responded to Sandi, I simply said, "I'm not in a good place. Can we talk later?" She said, "Thank you." When I was rested and in a better frame of mind later, I went downstairs and she said, "That was so helpful, because we're learning to communicate." There were no awkward feelings and we had a good day together.

Another passage reflecting a similar thought is found in James 4:1. "What causes quarrels and what causes fights among you? Is it not this, that your passions are at war within you?" When I am agitated and combative, the problem is not someone or something, it is inside me. My own passions are the root problem, and is where fights and quarrels begin. "Do you not see that whatever goes into the mouth passes into the stomach and is expelled? But what comes out of the mouth proceeds from the heart, and this defiles a person. For out of the heart come evil thoughts, murder, adultery, sexual immorality, theft, false witness, slander. These are what defile a person." (Matthew 15:17–20)

Passions are another word for our carnal nature. This passage is long, but worth reading, as it details the war within each of our hearts and beautifully articulates the conflict between a life of conflict and degradation in the flesh, and a life of peace and serenity in the Spirit.

"If you bite and devour one another, watch out that you are not consumed by one another. But I say, walk by the Spirit, and you will not gratify the desires of the flesh. For the desires of the flesh are against the Spirit, and the desires of the Spirit are against the flesh, for these are opposed to each other, to keep you from doing the things you want to do. But if you are led by the Spirit, you are not under the law. Now the works of the flesh are evident: sexual immorality, impurity, sensuality, idolatry, sorcery, enmity, strife, jealousy, fits of anger, rivalries, dissensions, divisions, envy, drunkenness, orgies, and things like these. I warn you, as I warned you before, that those who do such things will not inherit the kingdom of God. But the fruit of the Spirit is love, joy, peace, patience, kindness, goodness, faithfulness, gentleness, self-control; against such things there is no law. And those who belong to Christ Jesus have crucified the flesh with its passions and desires." (Galatians 5:15-24)

Instead of blaming other people for conflicts, I'm learning the first thing to do is assess the condition of my own spirit and heart. The problem is not the guy who cut me off in traffic, or the person who interrupted me, or the waiter who didn't treat me properly; the problem is usually in the mirror. How I respond to these situations makes me aware of the state of my spirit. If I am easily irritated, it is time to take a deep breath and seek God for a soft heart and a quiet spirit.

When I am bothered by other people, Jesus encourages me to embrace the aggravation as a teaching moment. "Why do you see the speck that is in your brother's eye, but do not notice the log that is in your own eye? Or, how can you say to your brother, 'Let me take the speck out of your eye,' when there is the log in your own eye? You hypocrite, first take the log out of your own eye, and then you will see clearly to take the speck out of your brother's eye." (Matthew 7:3-5)

Specks or splinters in someone else's eye are simply indicators I have a similar problem the size of a log in my own eye. When people push my buttons, it is an excellent opportunity to stop and ask God to reveal my own inadequacies before assuming everyone else is the problem.

I have observed an interesting dynamic in my own life. The more I am rooted and grounded in the love of God, the more willing I am to invite God to search my heart and reveal sources of pain. At the same time I am discovering there are painful experiences from my past hindering me from believing God unconditionally loves me. Confronting my pain and allowing God to continue to reveal His care and affection for me prompted me to write two other books, *Crisis to Christ* and *Knowing God's Love*. These two areas have been so instrumental in my personal healing and growth I could not summarize them in a mere chapter or two.

During our family business transition I found myself getting upset with other people who seemed to be conspiring against me. At one point I felt like I was completely alone and everyone was against me. I felt such pain I knew there was more going on deep inside me than what met the eye. I was so shaken I reached out to a group of friends for prayer and support and enlisted the help of professional therapists. I discovered the problem was in my own heart and was tied to pain from my past.

Several times God reminded me "flesh and blood" were not my enemies, but it sure felt like it then. In hindsight I am grateful for the difficult experience because it unearthed issues, which unresolved, would continue to emerge and harm others. I needed to confront my own problems and look at the huge logs in my own eye first.

Now I am in a much better place with God and able to listen to the input of those closest to me in a new way. A few years after this personal turning point, one of my sons and I had a several hour heart-to-heart talk. I learned how my actions had impacted him for many years. He told me each spring, around April, I would go through a dark time emotionally. He did not know what caused it, pressures of taxes being due, or increased work for the upcoming conference season, but from his perspective the whole family would hold their breath waiting for the inevitable outburst. When I did finally blow, he said I would quickly repent and apologize, but the damage had been done.

I will never forget those words. I remembered them the next spring when I sensed my wife was a little on edge and asked her about it. She simply said, "It's April," and my heart sank. How I wish I would have known then what I know now. Now that I am more aware of the effects of my pain, and my propensity to overwork, be stressed, and push myself too far, I consciously seek to rest and be careful not to push myself. This year we all made it through April without any outbursts or hurtful language. With my heart in a better place, my tongue followed suit.

As a Christian, I know out of the abundance of the heart, my mouth speaks. My speech reflects what I hold dear and the values I hold in my heart. When my heart is good, my tongue will be good. When my heart is agitated, my tongue is more prone to be sharp and caustic. My tongue does not operate on it's own, but is an extension of my heart. "The good person out of the good treasure of his heart produces good, and the evil person out of his evil treasure produces evil, for out of the abundance of the heart his mouth speaks." (Luke 6:45)

Prayer

Create in me a clean heart, O God, and renew a right spirit within me. let the words of my mouth and the meditation of my heart be acceptable in your sight, oh Lord my Rock and my Redeemer.
(These words are found in Psalm 19:14 and Psalm 51:10)

CHAPTER 3:
A QUIET HEART

Since the heart is the source of my speech I know I need to take whatever time I need to develop a quiet and tranquil heart. When I am calm; quiet, resting, trusting, teachable, soft, filled with the spirit, and at peace with God, then the ability to communicate well is virtually assured.

For most of my life, I received any input or feedback personally, which is why it was difficult for those who knew me best to tell me things I needed to hear. I've been learning this from my family. Having a consultant/counselor present in our family discussions enabled my wife and sons to give me input I should have heard a long time ago. I finally asked, "How come I haven't heard any of this before?" Because I would have taken it personally, which they all knew.

One reason I took input or criticism personally is because when anyone questioned my decisions or practices as a husband, father or businessman, they weren't disagreeing with what I had done, I thought they were attacking who I was. They were confronting my identity. If someone said "Using blocks to teach math is stupid" my head translated it "I am a stupid teacher." Who I was had become interwoven with how I performed. If my wife seemed happy, then I was satisfied. If my sons were okay, then this part of my life was okay. If customers and employees were content, then so was I. I wasn't finding my sense of who I was in God alone, but in how I was perceived.

As I have been learning to be rooted and grounded in Christ, I'm able to hear things I never could hear before. I'm realizing I'm not a businessman, I'm not a speaker, I'm not a dad, I'm not a husband, I'm an adopted child of God. Period. I also wear other hats and have multiple responsibilities, but I find my identity in being an unconditionally loved child of God. I am His son and He is my Dad.

What I do flows from who I am and not the reverse. Doing good things does not define me. Being a child of God does. The Spirit has made me know I'm God's kid. In several passages in Romans and Galatians, we are informed of the Spirit's work in witnessing with our spirit, God is our "Abba father" or "daddy."

"You did not receive the spirit of slavery to fall back into fear, but you have received the Spirit of adoption as sons, by whom we cry, "Abba! Father!" (Romans 8:15)

"Because you are sons, God has sent the Spirit of his Son into our hearts, crying, 'Abba! Father!'" (Galatians 4:6)

Instead of working hard to keep everyone happy, I am redirecting my energies to believing this fundamental truth and abiding in this knowledge – I am His and He is mine.

The most important part of my day has become the morning when I get close to my Dad and am reaffirmed I'm His son. In 2012 I discovered something. I found out my Heavenly Father not only loves me, He also likes me.

I heard the gospel for the first time when I was 14 years old at a Young Life Ranch in Colorado. I learned if I confessed my sins, and received Jesus as my savior, I could know Jesus personally, have my sins forgiven, and go to heaven when I died. Gradually, over the years, I started thinking somehow he'd like me more if I did more stuff for him, like reading my Bible each day.

I know this is bad theology and would've identified it as such, but even though my brain knew better, deep down in my heart I embraced this unbiblical thinking and believed His liking me, and being pleased with me, was tied to what I did.

It's a problem the Galatian church also had. They were tempted to believe in order to be accepted into the church, they needed to receive God's grace AND be circumcised. Today we have people who tell us we need to believe AND join their church, or be baptized, or be pro-life, or .... It seems there is always something more we have to do. While these are all worthwhile activities, if anything is added to grace, then it is not grace but works. I address this more in my book *Knowing God's Love*, but this will suffice for now.

God uses my son, John, a young man with Downs Syndrome, to teach me about the unconditional nature of grace and love. He asks me to shave him. He can shave himself, but he likes it when Pop does it. This young man thinks I'm the best thing since sliced bread. He doesn't know if I'm a good businessman or speaker. He doesn't know if I'm a fine husband or good father. I'm just his Pop. The first thing he does every morning is come downstairs and crawl up into my lap. Sometimes I don't really want a 160 pound man sitting in my lap with bad breath and in need of a shave, but I stop what I am doing and hug him back. He doesn't hug me in the traditional sense, he holds me.

Because of John's unconditional love for me, I started praying, "Lord I know you love me because you love the world and I'm part of the world, but I'd really like to believe you like me as much as my son likes me." God answered my prayer by showing me how much He loved me. Through sermons, scriptures, songs, and varied experiences, God revealed His love and affection for me.

Two of these passages are: "We love because he first loved us." (1 John 4:19) and "God shows his love for us in that while we were still sinners, Christ died for us." (Romans 5:8)

This knowledge finally made it's way from my head to my heart when it dawned on me one day, my Dad really likes me for who I am.

This morning, I reread the account of the prodigal son. I highlighted all the verses about the father; "And the father saw him afar off. The father with compassion ran down the street and embraced him." Luke 15:20 I study like this regularly because I still have a problem believing God really likes me. One morning I woke up and said, "Lord do you still love me as much today as you did yesterday?" You know what God said? Nothing.

He did give me a picture in my mind of Jesus, standing in the heavens with His arms spread wide, saying, "Of course I do. I don't have any baggage." When I get a mental picture or a vision I often ask, "Is this message biblical?" As I sought to discern the veracity of this illumination, the first thing I thought of was the father of the prodigal son running down the street.

He saw the pig smelling kid coming back, who had just lost half of his fortune, and instead of waiting for him to properly clean up and express repentance, the father ran down the street, probably losing a sandal in the process, with his robe flapping, and he grabbed his wayward son and said, "My boy!"

Then I remembered the verse, "God is love." (1 John 4:16) and "God is light, and in Him is no darkness at all." (1 John 1:5) Both of these passages came quickly to mind along with the concept that God never changes; He is the same "yesterday, today, and forever." (Hebrews 13:8) I concluded this illumination is biblically sound. I like the word "illuminate" because this picture is not only biblical it illuminates these truths to me in a fresh way.

Over the course of the past few years, I am learning the more I accept how much my Dad likes me for who I am, and know He is my Father, the better I'm able to relate to my wife and to communicate with her and anyone else. The more rooted and grounded I am in the love of God, the nicer I am to be around. The best thing I can do for our family is to spend time with my Dad, and let him love me, hold me, affirm me, and bring me to a place of peace.

There is a wonderful prayer I have used as a basis for my own prayer in Ephesians 3:14-19. "For this reason I bow my knees before the Father, from whom every family in heaven and on earth is named, that according to the riches of His glory He may grant you to be strengthened with power through His Spirit in your inner being, so that Christ may dwell in your hearts through faith—that you, being rooted and grounded in love, may have strength to comprehend with all the saints what is the breadth and length and height and depth, and to know the love of Christ that surpasses knowledge, that you may be filled with all the fullness of God."

It is a long passage but I have found it very helpful for my faith and my prayers. I am seeking God continually to be "strengthened with power through His Spirit' and be "rooted and grounded" and "comprehend with all the saints" the scope of the "love of Christ that surpasses knowledge." The more rooted and grounded I am in His love, the better equipped I am to have Godly communication.

Here is a list of fruits which follow a heart which is resting, settled, and at peace.

When my heart beats with God's heart, coupled with a healthy sense of my own integrity and identity, I am enabled to:

- Speak the truth accurately.
- Not have a need for erecting fences to protect myself.
- Not defend myself or take information personally.
- Thoughtfully respond and not react emotionally.
- Foster a safe atmosphere, where children are able to address difficult topics.
- Be faithful to the truth.
- Believe the best of the speaker.
- Create a safe place for open, honest, safe, communication.

These characteristics of speaking the truth in love, which is our aim, parallel the expressions of love in 1 Corinthians 13:4-6. I borrowed some phrases from the ESV and others from the NASB while adding the phrase "loving communication."

- Loving communication is patient and kind;
- Loving communication does not brag and is not arrogant;
- Loving communication does not act unbecomingly;
- Loving communication does not insist on its own way;
- Loving communication is not provoked;
- Loving communication does not take into account a wrong suffered;
- Loving communication rejoices with the truth.

- Loving communication bears all things, believes all things, hopes all things, endures all things.

Prayer

Father, strength me with power in my inner being through your Good Spirit. And may the Spirit of God pour into my heart the love of God and direct my heart to the love of God and to the steadfastness of Christ. In the name of Jesus the Christ, Amen. (Ephesians 3:16, Romans 5:5, and 2 Thessalonians 3:5)

CHAPTER 4: ESTEEM ONE ANOTHER HIGHLY

In this section, I'm thinking primarily of communicating with my wife, but this principle applies to everyone. I have not done well in esteeming or counting her more significant than myself. This language and this way of thinking is used in the inspired letter to the Philippian church in which we are encouraged to have this mindset exemplified in Jesus.

"Do nothing from selfish ambition or conceit, but in humility count others more significant than yourselves. Let each of you look not only to his own interests, but also to the interests of others. Have this mind among yourselves, which is yours in Christ Jesus, who, though He was in the form of God, did not count equality with God a thing to be grasped, but emptied Himself, by taking the form of a servant, being born in the likeness of men. And being found in human form, He humbled himself by becoming obedient to the point of death, even death on a cross." (Philippians 2:3-8)

I have been guilty of treating Sandi as a second-class citizen. I had misinterpreted and misapplied passages teaching about submission and helpmeets as inferring women were subservient by nature and I was wrong. I am not addressing roles, which is a different topic, I am focusing on how I viewed my wife.

I learned this from the lips of my wife. One evening she quietly informed me that many times she has felt like I treated her without mutuality and respect. Sadly I acknowledge she was accurate and my attitude reflected my beliefs. "For as he thinks within himself, so he is." (Proverbs 23:7)

My speech reflects my beliefs and reflects my values and theological underpinnings. If I am going to treat Sandi in a way which reflects Christ, then I have to think of her like Christ thinks of her. My wife was created in the image of God. She was given to me by God. God designed her to be one flesh with me. She is a valued member of the Church with gifts and talents to uniquely build up the body of Christ. She is also a joint heir and an adopted child of God.

The more I think scripturally about this special and unique individual, the easier it is to esteem her highly and treat her well. She's an incredible woman of God. She's wonderful. She has home educated four sons, one of whom has a disability. She has been a pastor's wife, an incredible helpmeet, a daughter who has honored her parents, and a steadfast servant of Christ who has followed Jesus faithfully since she was a child.

As I embrace this belief system, my speech will reflect my convictions because my mind, heart, and tongue are all connected. Biblical God-honoring thinking precedes and fosters biblical God-honoring communication.

A significant part of my problem was misunderstanding biblical authority. The disciples also misunderstood authority. Jesus gave them some direct teaching on the topic. "You know that the rulers of the Gentiles lord it over them, and their great ones exercise authority over them. It shall not be so among you. But whoever would be great among you must be your servant." (Matthew 20:26) In the kingdom of men, people in authority rule over others, but in the kingdom of God people who have been given positions of leadership are to serve others.

Jesus not only taught this doctrine to those who were to be the first apostles and leaders of the church, He lived this doctrine. He gave them an example of this kind of serving when He washed their feet. "Jesus, knowing that the Father had given all things into His hands, and that He had come from God and was going back to God, rose from supper. He laid aside His outer garments, and taking a towel, tied it around His waist. Then He poured water into a basin and began to wash the disciples' feet and to wipe them with the towel that was wrapped around Him." (John 13:3–5)

"When He had washed their feet and put on His outer garments and resumed His place, He said to them, "Do you understand what I have done to you? You call me Teacher and Lord, and you are right, for so I am. If I then, your Lord and Teacher, have washed your feet, you also ought to wash one another's feet. For I have given you an example, that you also should do just as I have done to you." (John 13:12–15)

Paul reminded believers in Corinth about "the authority that the Lord has given me for building up and not for tearing down." (2 Corinthians 13:10) In God's kingdom, the normal ways of operating are often reversed. God has given authority to serve and to build up, not to rule over or tear down. As a husband and father I was guilty of misusing my authority. I now am committed to building up and serving those who are within the sphere of my influence, for this is what God created and designed me to do.

As in all teaching, there is a balance. While I have incorrectly thought too highly of myself, there may be others who think too lowly of themselves. Since we are each children of God, created in His image, with inherent value and a gift to contribute to the body of Christ, we each are worthy of being heard. For those who speak too much and think too highly of their insights and thoughts, a little humility may be just what they need. For those who lack confidence in their gifting and what they have been providentially equipped to provide to others, maybe a little spunk and initiative is needed.

This verse covers both bases: "By the grace given to me I say to everyone among you not to think of himself more highly than he ought to think, but to think with sober judgment, each according to the measure of faith that God has assigned." (Romans 12:3) We need to think soberly and honestly. Not too high, and not too low, but according to the faith God has assigned to each of His children.

Esteem Everyone

In 2006 our family attended our first Joni and Friends Family Retreat. Even though we have a son with Downs Syndrome, this was the first time we had been to a camp where every family included someone who was effected by a disability. For the first few days I saw the outward signs of disability. But after a few days, I began to see the real person. I didn't see the wheelchair; I saw the man. I didn't see the speech impediment, but got to know the heart of the individual.

The highlight of the camp was the talent show when each person had a chance to shine. Some would sing, some would act, and some would play a musical instrument. Others would share a significant event which happened in the past year or read a meaningful poem they had written. Jane was a lady who had difficulty speaking and was confined to a wheelchair, but I learned she had authored several books of poetry. David has cerebral palsy which affects his muscles and is also in a wheelchair, and he taught himself sign language with a video program so he could communicate with his best friend. He signed and did an amazing job performing a praise song. Each of these people have value, and I am to count them more highly than myself. The more I got to know them, the easier Romans 12:3 was to apply.

Whether we are listening to our wife, or someone affected with a disability, or the youngest member of the family, we need to treat them with love and respect.

Good Godly communication begins with two people who esteem each other highly, honor each other, and respect each other. This is really the golden rule, isn't it? Treating others as we hope to be treated. If while I'm speaking to somebody or when I'm listening to someone, I value this person and count them more significant than myself, my communication will be transformed. As parents model this kind of honorable communication, it will rub off on their children.

Before we open our mouths we need to have our hearts resting and calm, and our minds thinking biblically. Only God can help us here. Let's seek Him.

Prayer

Father, help me to esteem others highly and value others as more significant than myself. Give me the mind of Christ, be present in my thinking, and be glorified in my speaking. I ask in the name of the Servant King Jesus, amen.

CHAPTER 5:
CREATE A
SAFE PLACE

If I had the opportunity to start over as a husband and father, a do-over if you will, the number one thing I would seek to be is gentle and kind. My goal would be to have a safe home where everybody could be who God designed them to be without fear of what I might say or how I would react. I would use the "the authority that the Lord has given me for building up and not for tearing down" (2 Corinthians 13:10) for building up and encouraging those who are closest to me.

My greatest desire is to be like Jesus. I would like to be approachable, gentle, and meek like my Lord. I'm six foot five, weigh an eighth of a ton, and can be very intimidating. My hope and prayer is for my granddaughters, my wife, and my children feel comfortable around me. I don't want them to be wondering if I have had enough sleep, or if I am going to be angry, or if they have to walk on eggshells, waiting for a disruption.

The safest man to speak with would be Jesus. In Matthew 12:18-20 we have an insightful description of the Son of God. "Behold, my servant whom I have chosen, my beloved with whom my soul is well pleased. I will put my Spirit upon Him, and He will proclaim justice to the Gentiles. He will not quarrel or cry aloud, nor will anyone hear His voice in the streets; a bruised reed He will not break, and a smoldering wick He will not quench." An illustration is used to describe Jesus which is hard to understand in our modern culture.

I assume a reed is a thin, fragile piece of wood placed in the end of a clarinet. Smoking wick sounds like a flickering candle about to expire. Apparently Jesus was not loud or boisterous for He did not cry aloud or quarrel. He was also careful not to crush a fragile object or extinguish a candle about to go out. He was safe to be with. Your spirit would not be crushed, extinguished, or bruised in His presence.

Because Jesus is a safe person, we are in a safe place when we are near Him. "Come to me, all who labor and are heavy laden, and I will give you rest. Take my yoke upon you, and learn from me, for I am gentle and lowly in heart, and you will find rest for your souls. For my yoke is easy, and my burden is light." (Matthew 11:28–30)

I want Sandi's spirit to be able to rest when we are together. I want to encourage her and not quench her spirit. I don't want to blow out her candle but fan its flame so it burns more brightly.

Two important verses to me in this regard are John 15:9 and 12. Jesus is speaking, "As the Father has loved me, so have I loved you." Then He says a few verses later, "As I have loved you, love each other." He's not telling me to just love my wife this way, but everybody. We are to love people as we have been loved.

How did Jesus love me? With this concept as my guide, I think about how Jesus loved and loves me. Since Jesus is God, and God is love, then Jesus is love. To help me flesh out how Jesus loves, I made a slight modification to 1 Corinthians 13. "Jesus is patient, and kind. Jesus does not envy or boast. He's not arrogant or rude." In another version, Jesus is not irritable or resentful. Jesus rejoices with the truth. Jesus bears all things, believes all things, hopes all things, endures all things.

We could also amplify this concept by placing our own name at the end of each phrase. Jesus is patient to Steve. Jesus is kind to Steve. Jesus does not envy or boast with Steve. Jesus is not arrogant or rude with Steve. Jesus is not irritable or resentful with Steve. This is your first homework assignment, make a list of these attributes and put your name at the end. This is how Jesus loves each of us. This helps me know how I am to love others.

As Jesus is to me, I desire to be for my wife. I want to be patient and kind. The hardest part of 2012 was having a consultant at the table, providing an environment where my wife and sons were free to have a voice. As each member of my family spoke, I learned I had been hurting those closest to me through things I had said and through attitudes I had adopted. This painful revelation was almost more than I could assimilate.

I no longer have a strong desire to build big things and do great deeds, I do want to be thoughtful, quick to hear, and slow to speak. I want to create a safe place in my home where my wife and my sons can freely express their opinions, embrace different convictions from my own, and feel heard, valued, and safe. Do I agree with my kids and my wife on everything? No. I still have strong convictions. I am learning I can have my own convictions without hurting people. This is the message of Romans 14:5 "Each one should be fully convinced in his own mind." In verse 19 Paul adds, "Let us pursue what makes for peace and for mutual upbuilding."

Our Family Code

One way our family tried to ensure our communication would be open, honest, and safe, was to develop a Communication Code of Conduct. Before every family board meeting we opened with prayer and then read the code. The chairman for the day then designated a sheriff to make sure we all adhered to these principles. Most of the points are common sense, but the process of developing them and then intentionally reading them at the beginning of each meeting kept them in the forefront of our thinking.

Demme Learning Communication Code of Conduct
1.   Listen and provide each other space
2.   Don't interrupt
3.   Full participation giving safe and honest feedback without fear
4.   Watch our tone of voice
5.   Ask for clarification
6.   Ask for time to process information and emotions when necessary
7.   Try not to personalize (keep it professional and above the line)

8. Define a clear agenda for meetings with advance notice
9. Ask for feedback
10. Process out loud
11. Avoid ultimatums
12. Share your thoughts and feelings openly (come to the line)
13. Use a process manager (sheriff)

We used this code for several years. As I grow in my understanding of speaking the turn in love, I continue to tweak and make changes to it. These principles re universal and not only apply to board meetings but everyday family situations as well. I will expand on these principles in the ensuing chapters.

Prayer

Father, fix our eyes on Jesus. Fill us with the Spirit of Jesus. Let the aroma of the gentle, kind, meek, and patient savior permeate our conversations. In Jesus' name, amen.

CHAPTER 6:
SPEAK THE TRUTH
IN LOVE

In this chapter we will discuss multiple techniques to consider when engaging in heart-to-heart conversations. In any dialogue, both the speaker and listener have work to do. We've already discussed the importance of self-awareness and being aware of the state of one's heart. Ideally, both parties are rested and willing to speak clearly and listen with respect. "Speaking the truth in love, we are to grow up in every way into him who is the head, into Christ," (Ephesians 4:15)

Tips for the Speaker
1 Watch Your Tone
2 Communicating for Clarity
3 The Pen
4 Be Emotionally Honest and Real
5 Avoid the Bully Pulpit
6 Don't Overstate Your Convictions
7 Look in the Mirror
8 Foster an Atmosphere of Mutual Respect

Watch your Tone
My counselor Steve, the one who was also my teacher, once said, "When I counsel a couple, I don't listen to what they say, I listen to how they say it." His observation astounded me. I had always thought

the content was the most important ingredient of speaking. Yet he had observed the tone in which someone is speaking is more revealing of what is going on in the relationship.

Speak the truth, and do it with love. Let your tone convey you are not angry or hurt, but speaking in a way which is controlled and thoughtful. "If you claim to be religious but don't control your tongue, you are fooling yourself." (James 1:26)

Jesus not only spoke the truth, He also was gracious. "Mercy and truth are met together; righteousness and peace have kissed each other." (Psalms 85:10 ASV)

in the gospel of John this language is used; "grace and truth came through Jesus Christ." (John 1:17)

Watching one's tone is more than not raising your voice or speaking harshly, it is speaking the truth, with grace and mercy as well.

Have a sense of reflection in your tone of voice and an openness, as if you are simply sharing information. Avoid sarcasm or using the opportunity to sermonize. If possible, keep your communication light and employ some humor.

Communicating for Clarity

The hardest principle for me is communicating for clarity and understanding, rather than convincing or persuading. As a Christian, this is almost counter intuitive. When I meet someone who is not a believer, I am generally praying and looking for an opportunity to share the Good News of Jesus.

As a result of this mentality, which is admirable to a degree, I'm not dialed in to what someone else is thinking and feeling, as much as I am looking for openings to interject truth. The reality is, I believe I do know the truth and have a responsibility to preach the gospel. But this is not what I am addressing in this seminar. The prime objective of two-way communication is not to change the way someone thinks but to understand what they think.

The Pen

One strategy our family has used is having a physical object for the speaker to hold. Having this object clarifies the speaker has the floor. We have used a pen, a salt shaker, and a wooden stick from Africa. Having the pen authorizes the speaker to speak without any interruption.

The possessor of the pen represents himself or herself. The speaker may use lots of personal pronouns such as "I," "me," and "my," "I feel," "I've observed," and "I think." The speaker strives to express as clearly as possible, what they are thinking and feeling. Their job is not to make a convincing argument or change the listener's opinion, but to speak the truth, accurately and plainly.

If you are speaking, represent yourself and talk as you would want to be talked to if you were the listener. If you can, take off your salesman hat which is trying to get the customer to agree with what you are saying. You are simply attempting to be open, honest, and gracious regardless of how the listener is reacting to what you are saying. You are communicating for clarity.

Several years ago I was present at a meeting of family members. There were seven siblings from around the country, who had not been together in one room for years. We were discussing the estate of their parents, a discussion which had the potential to be explosive. We gathered around the dining room table, and I suggested we use a saltshaker to help with our discussion. Whoever had the saltshaker had the floor. Everyone got on board with this idea, and it worked. Holding the saltshaker gave people permission to express themselves without fear of being interrupted, stifled, or intimidated by an older sibling.

Younger siblings expressed themselves clearly and with confidence. Some of them had been influenced and bullied by an older sibling their entire life. For the rest of the afternoon, one after another of the family members asked for the saltshaker and took turns talking until everybody had a chance to express their thoughts.

In our home, when my wife has the pen, she has the floor, and she is going to be able to express herself fully. When she has finished talking, while still holding the pen, I will ask questions to clarify or restate what she has said, to see if I heard her accurately. Or I might ask her to expand on several key words she mentioned. I'm not going to judge her, or decide if I agree with what she believes, or debate what she has stated. My goal is to hear her and understand her.

Be Emotionally Honest and Real

In addition to beginning sentences with personal pronouns, also share how you are feeling by saying "I feel." Then follow this phrase with one word adverbs such as "afraid," "nervous," "hopeful," "happy" or other words to describe what is going on in your own person.

A few years ago I had to a go through a difficult lawsuit. One evening, while I was out of state, Sandi texted me and asked how I was doing. In the past I would have said "Fine," but I am learning to be intellectually and emotionally honest. Instead of cutting the conversation short with "Fine," I texted her back and said, "I'm a little relieved, feeling a little vulnerable, a little wounded, and I'm sad." She replied "Thank you for letting me in." When I am open, transparent, vulnerable, and real, with Sandi our relationship grows and deepens.

I have probably lied thousands of times by saying I was fine when I wasn't. When people ask me, "How are you doing?" or "How are you?" and I answer, "Fine," when I am not, I am being honest. I'm taking this simple query very seriously now. When I was going through my tough time in 2012, friends would inquire, "How are you doing?" I would look at them and say, "Do you want to know?" If they hesitated, I knew they didn't want to know, and I would respond, "I'm doing," which is honest.

But if they said "Yes," and were genuinely interested, I would tell them. When I shared my story, and was emotionally honest, they felt free to share how they were feeling as well. We all spoke with integrity. I hardly had a shallow conversation for about two years because when I was open, others became open, and we experienced sincere fellowship and a heart connection.

I would like to add a little postscript on the response "Fine." I have the privilege of teaching about principles of communication. If the audience is comprised of men and women, I like to ask the ladies what feel like when their husband tells them they are fine. Their responses include: "shut out," "he doesn't want to tell me how he is feeling," "helpless," and "not good enough to talk to."

As a man, when I say "Fine," I am not trying to shut out my wife, I think I am being noble by sucking it up and sparing my wife having to hear about my personal struggles. What really happens when I respond with "Fine" is I create distance between my wife and myself. She feels at arm's length and excluded from my personal life. I think I am taking the high road and helping her, but the exact opposite message is conveyed.

Many people assume men answer "Fine" because they are unable to express their emotions. This is bunk. Men have emotional muscles, but when we do not use them and work on articulating the emotions we are experiencing, they become atrophied from lack of use. The book of Psalms, many of which were written by David, the warrior King, the lover of God, are replete with expressions of how David was feeling. He was honest and raw when talking to God.

Consider the emotions and feelings expressed by David in Psalm 6. He didn't put a brave face on and hide his thoughts. He wrote what he was experiencing as a prayer to God. He was real, transparent, and true to himself. "My soul also is greatly troubled. But you, O Lord— how long?" (Psalm 6:3) "I am weary with my moaning; every night I flood my bed with tears; I drench my couch with my weeping. My eye wastes away because of grief; it grows weak because of all my foes." (Psalm 6:6-7)

In Psalm 13:1-2 David is filled with sorrow because it seems God has forgotten him, "How long, O Lord? Will you forget me forever? How long will you hide your face from me? How long must I take counsel in my soul and have sorrow in my heart all the day?"

Avoid the Bully Pulpit

The expression Bully Pulpit was first used by Theodore Roosevelt when he was president. During his presidency, in the first years of the 20th century, "bully" had a different meaning than it does today. It was used to describe something as really great, a good thing. The term "Bully Pulpit" means a position of authority enabling one to promote personal views or agenda. As president, he used his unique position to put forth his political platform.

As a father, God has given me authority to serve, build up, encourage, and train my children. I have misused this position by expressing my thoughts on a wide variety of topics and assuming my family shared my opinions as well. I learned I came close to hurting my children without knowing it.

When my sons went off to college they had an opportunity to think and examine life for themselves. One of my sons attended the services of a different denomination each Sunday for several months to hear what they taught. He was searching and developing his own convictions, which I applaud. I have always wanted my sons to be seekers of truth like the Bereans, those people who lived in Berea described by Luke in Acts 17:11, "Now these were more noble than those in Thessalonica, in that they received the word with all readiness of the mind, examining the scriptures daily, whether these things were so." They heard Paul and then examined the scriptures themselves to see if his message was accurate.

During a Christmas break, one of my sons got up his courage to tell me he had a crisis of sorts in his personal beliefs because he met someone from a different political persuasion than me, who was not only a believer but a nice man. This shocked him because he assumed from the way I spoke about people of this stripe, they would be almost evil and it shook him to wonder what other misinformation I had taught him. He told me, "Pop, if you had explained why you believed what you believed, that would have been so helpful. You assumed, because we lived in the same home with you we would adopt all of your convictions. We didn't know why you were pro-life, and why you thought government should be limited, and why you called yourself a conservative.

But if you had explained this from scripture or your own experiences, this would have helped us to understand you."

I learned the hard way from my son's comments. 1 Peter 3:15 says, "Always be prepared to make a defense to anyone who asks you for a reason for the hope that is in you; yet do it with gentleness and respect." My son helped me realize I had been lazy in my training, failing to explain from scripture the reasoning behind my beliefs. Nor had I done a good job of responding with "gentleness and respect" to those who didn't agree with my positions. Fortunately I have watched each of my sons grow and mature and they are much better than I was at thinking through what they believe and articulating their beliefs honestly, and with gentleness and respect. I think they have inherited this propensity from their mom!

Don't Overstate your Convictions

Absolutely every story sounds a million times better when the facts are embellished and exaggerated by the speaker. Absolutely every one? A million times better? Be accurate and honest. Speak the truth, nothing more and nothing less. When you use this time of discussion as a platform for making a point, then you will be tempted to stretch the truth to support your position. If you are not trying to win an argument or convince someone of your position, but are simply representing yourself and seeking clarity, then this will not be a problem.

"Let what you say be simply 'Yes' or 'No'; anything more than this comes from evil." (Matthew 5:37)

Look in the Mirror

When you speak, think about how you look when you are communicating. Consider looking in the mirror once in awhile. You might not know how you look when you process what is being said.

Sandi is an introvert. When she is assimilating information, she processes and thinks thorough what she hears. She needs time to chew on and digest new information. While she is processing, she is not aware of her facial signals. She is concentrating on what she has learned.

On the other hand, I am an extrovert and an open book. People who speak to me know pretty much what I am thinking. I also process information quickly and can formulate a response to what is being asked of me in a short time. I think quickly on my feet.

As a speaker and teacher, I also read faces and look for clues to see how my presentation is being received. I've spent years as a preacher, taught in many classrooms, and sat across the table from students who I was tutoring. I can look at an audience and have a pretty good idea of who is struggling, who is being moved, and who wishes they were not present. I'm also learning I can't read introverts as well as I thought, because introverts are focused on processing, and thinking things through and I probably won't really discover what they think until the next day.

One day, after I had just spoken at a conference, Sandi complimented me on my presentation. I thought "Really?" Because I was watching her throughout the session and her face was conveying she didn't like what I had said. Now her mouth was saying she liked the talk. I was unable to reconcile the inconsistency between her facial expression and her words. I puzzled over this disparity for years.

My family is learning to apply these principles, so a short while ago I said something and as Sandi was processing how to respond she quit smiling. I wondered what had upset her and I had a puzzled expression on my face. She saw my bewilderment, thought about the mirror and said "Don't move."

She walked into the bathroom and looked at herself in the mirror. Then she emerged and said, "I'm sorry. I understand why you think I'm reacting to what you said, but it's just my face. My face is telling you something I'm not really thinking. I'm just processing." After being flummoxed for years, the mystery of the facial disparity was finally solved.

This situation may be totally reversed in your home. Perhaps the husband is the introvert and the wife is the extrovert. You will figure these things out as you talk to each other. You might even say, "I'm really sorry, I'm getting two messages. Your words are not lining up with your face, can you help me?" The same may hold true for the facial expressions of your children.

Foster an Atmosphere of Mutual Respect

When I was going through a dark time in 2012, which corresponded to a bad time for my wife and sons, I sought the help of a therapist. This was something I didn't think I would ever choose. "I'll never go to a shrink. I can figure this out myself" was my mantra. During one of our sessions, the counselor asked Sandi if there was something she would like to tell me which would be difficult for me to hear. She said , "There is one thing I could never tell Steve, because he would die if he knew what I think."

She went on to say, "I have lived with this man for thirty years, I know what he thinks."

I had never been silent on my convictions about church, education, or politics. I made them known to everybody within my home, and anybody else who would listen. Our therapist said, "Why don't you try?" So she took a deep breath and trotted it out. Having a third party present provided the safety she needed. After a brief silence, the counselor looked at me for a response and I said, "Still breathing."

Do I agree with my wife on this particular subject? No, she's absolutely right. I don't agree with her, but I heard her. I am valuing her opinion even though I don't share it. You might say, "This is basic stuff." For me, this is huge. My responsibility is not to fix people or change the way they think. Change and transformation is God's department. My calling is to love them, understand them, and remain faithful and honest with what God has revealed to me.

I used to prefer associating with people who believed what I believed. I had strong convictions about this. Now I'm learning there are probably no two people in the world who agree on every single point. I have to remind myself we are all created in the image of God and we all have value. I'm learning for the first time to listen with respect to people with whom I don't agree.

After years of practice, Sandi and I can now talk about pretty much anything. If you have never gotten to the place where you can talk about difficult and important matters, get a consultant or therapist. For the first two years of our family business we always had a consultant present at board meetings. It created a safe place for everybody in the room.

I have listed these eight points to help in communicating with grace and clarity. Feel free to make your own list and make changes as you grow in your ability to speak well.

"Set a guard, O LORD, over my mouth; keep watch over the door of my lips!" (Psalms 141:3)

"Let your speech always be gracious, seasoned with salt, so that you may know how you ought to answer each person." Colossians 4:6

Prayer

Father keep a watch over my mouth and let my speech be gracious and seasoned with salt. Enable me to speak the truth with love. In the precious name of Jesus, amen.

CHAPTER 7:
QUICK TO HEAR AND
SLOW TO SPEAK

Tips for the Listener
1. Listen Without Interrupting
2. Provide Undivided Attention
3. Value the Speaker
4. Listen without Personalizing
5. Rule Your Spirit
6. Stay at the Table
7. Take a Time-out
8. Follow Through

The primary responsibility of the listener is to listen carefully and hear what the speaker is communicating. Whether you agree with what is being said is not the point. The number one goal is to understand what the speaker is saying. As the listener, I need to be rested and at peace. I want to hear and understand what is being said regardless of whether I agree or not. I want to value the speaker and their words. My aim is to treat the presenter as I would want to be treated if I were speaking.

Listen without Interrupting
When it is my turn to listen and I have relinquished the pen(from the previous chapter), I am trusting God to help me be "quick to hear, slow to speak." (James 1:19) When a speaker opens his heart and entrusts

you with truths and insights into his being, we have to receive what has been said carefully. The speaker is vulnerable and much more liable to be wounded when his guard has been let down.

Provide Undivided Attention

If Sandi is going to invest time to speak to me, then as the listener I choose to turn off my cellphone and any other electronics. I am not going to check any social media. I want to face her when she is speaking, focus, and maintain positive eye contact, occasionally nodding, affirming, and expressing interest in what is being spoken.

We have a dear friend who is on the autism spectrum. Eye contact is hard for him. He can listen well without looking at the speaker, which is natural for him. He has learned looking directly at people when they are talking to him is important. He makes the effort to do what is not easy for him because he is thinking of others. In this tangible way, he is valuing them.

While I am seeking to hear and understand Sandi, there will be no deep breaths, no sighing, no sucking my lips, no rolling my eyes, nor interrupting. In other words I am to apply the second commandment and treat her like I want to be treated when it's my turn with the pen. I'm giving her respect. I'm esteeming her highly.

Value the Speaker

Before I make a snap judgement and speak based

on my quick analysis, I have found I need time to pause to really hear what I have heard and value what the speaker is thinking, feeling, or expressing.

I need to intentionally remember the principles of esteeming one another highly covered in chapter 4. Knowing the speaker is a child of God, created in His image, a member of the body of Christ, with unique value and a spiritual gift, helps me to focus and listen with all of my attention. The speaker is not inferior, but my brother or sister in Christ.

Another strategy which helps me is considering how I would like to be listened to if I were speaking. This is treating others like I want to be treated. I want to be heard, understood, and valued regardless of what I believe. I want to be listened to with respect.

Listen without Personalizing

When we first began having family business discussions I was surprised and shocked how personally I would take any comments I perceived were critical of how I had run the company to this point. I thought I was big enough to hear what everyone had to say, but found out I was the most susceptible to being offended. Since I learned these skills in the context of our family discussions, I am now applying them to my times of talking with Sandi.

One of the highlights of our marriage communication occurred about two years ago. Sandi began the conversation by saying "I have something to talk about today, which is going to be hard for you to hear, but it worked out okay." First of all, this is a thoughtful way to start a conversation which has the potential to be painful. It made me know what I was about to hear might hurt me to hear it, but she was at peace with how it ended.

In the past when Sandi would say, "I need to talk," I would immediately become defensive. Do all men respond similarly? When we did sit down, I was only about ten percent present. Even though I was outwardly calm and engaged, ninety percent of my brain was desperately assembling my defense team. I was contacting my lawyers, I had my research people on full alert, and I was scanning my internal hard drive wondering, "where did I mess up?"

I figured I was in trouble for something I had done and and I was scrambling to figure out what it was, because I'm going to be on the stand soon. Today, I am in a much better place than ever before. I'm much more rooted and grounded in Christ alone. The phrase, "rooted and grounded," is found in Paul's prayer for the Ephesian believers, "According to the riches of his glory he may grant you to be strengthened with power through his Spirit in your inner being, so that Christ may dwell in your hearts through faith—that you, being rooted and grounded in love may have strength to comprehend with all the saints what is the breadth and length and height and depth, and to know the love of Christ that surpasses knowledge, that you may be filled with all the fullness of God." (Ephesians 3:16–19)

I still take input and correction personally, as I'm still human, but not nearly as often as the first thirty years of our marriage. So while my wife was speaking on this occasion, I was all there. I was one hundred percent focused on what she was about to say. I didn't have any defense team, there were no lawyers on call, nothing.

She began to talk about a painful experience. As she shared it, I was fully present. I understood her and even felt some of her pain. I empathized to the point where I teared up while she was speaking. When she was finished speaking, I said, "Oh, I'm so sorry, that must have really hurt." Because I was fully present, I understood her as I never had before. After she picked up her jaw from the floor, she replied, "Wow, you really heard me." Thanks to these principles I am hearing and understanding her as never before.

Rule Your Spirit

If you decide what you are upset about is something to overlook, then do so without carrying around an attitude. If you need to address it, take responsibility to do so with clarity so no one has to wonder or guess, what you are thinking. It is better to express your emotions than to allow them to escalate and explode.

"Whoever is slow to anger is better than the mighty, and he who rules his spirit than he who takes a city." (Proverbs 16:32) One thing I know is if I am hungry, tired, or on edge, my spirit will not be easy to control. As humans we are spiritual, physical, emotional creatures. Our emotions impact our body. Our spirits are affected by our emotions, etc. We are "fearfully and wonderfully made." (Psalm 139:14) We are also fragile and easily broken. "We have this treasure in jars of clay, to show that the surpassing power belongs to God and not to us." (2 Corinthians 4:7) If I am not taking care of my jar of clay I will not be able to speak well or listen carefully.

Stay at the Table

Avoid ultimatums, tantrums, and the explosive power play when you are upset. I was at a family business meeting when some hard stuff was coming across the table and our consultant said to me, "Steve, I have seen so many fathers at this juncture, who will just pound the table and say 'I don't need this' and walk out of the room, and their family will probably never recover." He knew I was struggling but he affirmed me for staying at the table and not walking away when I was tempted to do so.

When your buttons have been triggered, verbalize it. Say "I am hurting" or "I need some space." Let the people at the table know what has been said has touched you deeply and you need a time-out to process the words.

The temptation for me, when I was hurting, was to make extreme statements and issue ultimatums. I am sad and ashamed to confess this. I have since learned anger and power plays are not conducive to honest and open communication. We need to be careful. We may not necessarily be feeling anger, but we use it as a tool to get our way and to create separation when we are on the hot seat. Sometimes the reason we get angry is just because people are getting a little too close to the truth, and we are feeling vulnerable. Don't let anger drive those closest to you away.

When I think of staying at the table and not leaving the room I also think about staying engaged emotionally as well. I know it is possible for me to be physically present but emotionally absent. I want to be present in body and spirit and not check out when the going gets rough.

Take a Time-out

If you need time to process and assimilate information you have heard, or to discern your emotions, ask for a time-out. This takes maturity and being comfortable in your own skin and sense of who you are in Christ. We have discovered talking about difficult problems can affect each person differently. It is hard to predict how some piece of information will be received by everyone in the room. Give each other space and don't assume you know how each person will respond or react.

If you feel like you are going to react after an emotional button has just been triggered, verbalize what you are experiencing, call for a short recess. You may only need a few minutes to breathe deeply or go for a short walk to restore peace in your spirit. Say "Wow, that was hard for me to hear and I think I need a few minutes to process this information." Or "I need some space. Could we have a short break so I can collect myself?"

A few chapters ago I shared how I responded when my wife awoke all perky and full of joy and I was exhausted after the long drive to the wedding. I knew no matter what she said, I was going to react emotionally. I was fragile, and I was aware of my own condition. I needed time to rest before I could respond thoughtfully. This is why I said, "I'm not in a good place and need some space." I was essentially asking for a time-out.

Follow Through

If you are unable to overcome your anxiety and need more time, come back to the room and tell how you are feeling. Suggest postponing this discussion for another day? But don't leave this open-ended, get out your calendar and set a time and place.

If Sandi tells me something difficult to hear and I am too tired to follow through then, I don't want to say let's talk about it at another time without setting a specific time. If I say let's talk about some other time then I am not valuing her or what she has said. If I say, "When can we address this again and make an appointment" I am conveying respect for her and our relationship.

Prayer

Father give me grace to be a thoughtful gracious listener. Help me to value the speaker, and listen carefully to what is being said. Give me ears to hear, in Jesus' name amen.

CHAPTER 8:
CLARIFY FOR
UNDERSTANDING

Tips for clarification

1 Affirm and Acknowledge
2 Ask, Don't Assume
3 Inquire
4 Explore Key Words
5 Restate
6 The Gift of Being Heard

Affirm and Acknowledge

Even though the speaker may be finished talking, the listener's work is not yet finished. This next step, we will call 'clarify for understanding,' begins with a quick summary of what you heard, humbly asking if you heard correctly what was just shared. You might begin your remarks by saying "thank you for sharing," even if you don't agree with what has been said. Affirm the person speaking and say, "I get what you are saying, and I appreciate your insights and courage for speaking." It doesn't mean you endorse what they said, but you are appreciating them.

I have never had the privilege of going to an AA meeting, but I have attended a joint meeting of AA folks with church people. I admire their candor, courage, and honesty. A person will stand up and say, "Hi, I'm Joe." Everybody politely responds, "Hi, Joe." After they have given their testimony everyone will say, "Thank you for sharing." And he sits down.

If people were to be brutally honest at a Christian prayer meeting, what might happen? As soon as they were finished speaking, well-meaning folks would be trying to help, praying over them, giving them a book, or connecting with them by sharing how they had a similar problem and how God healed them. Why would anyone want to open themselves up in this kind of environment? I wouldn't. Perhaps this is why we are so superficial in our sharing of needs. We can be helped to death. I think there is a lot we can learn from AA. God help us to be open and honest and say, "Thank you for sharing. I hear you. I understand you." I believe the AA approach is closer to the spirit of "bearing each others burdens" in the New Testament.

We are not trying to fix people but understand them. This is the prime directive, as a Star Trek officer would gently remind us.

Ask, Don't Assume

After the speaker has finished the presentation, you have listened well, and before the pen is handed to you, for your turn to speak, ask questions to clarify and explore what has been said. The primary objective for the listener is to truly hear what has been said. "You do not have, because you do not ask." (James 4:2)

My mind works very quickly. This can be an asset and a liability. In this area of listening I have to consciously not allow my mind to jump to conclusions based on the impressions I gathered hearing what the speaker had to say for the first time. I need to ask questions to find out more accurately what has been communicated. I do this by asking questions, exploring key words, and restating what I heard. This is not natural for me. But the fruit of the Spirit is "self-control." (Galatians 5:23) The Spirit helps me pause and listen to understand better than I ever could left to my own devices.

In Joshua 22:10-30 their is a potential civil war about to break out. The two and a half tribes were returning to the lands east of the Jordan River, having fulfilled their obligation to fight with their countrymen until the land was securely in the hands of the Israelites. The had built an altar to establish their kinship with the nine and a half tribes, but it was misunderstood and an army had been sent to quell the rebellion.

There are two lessons to be learned in this account. The first is before the battle was joined, Phinehas the priest asked the heads of the Transjordan tribes what was the meaning of the altar, even though they thought they knew. When they heard the response, war was averted and reconciliation occurred.

The second lesson concerns their response. These men from Reuben, Gad, and the half-tribe of Manasseh did not react, they carefully responded. Their soft answer turned away the wrath of the leaders of the other tribes. "A soft answer turns away wrath, but a harsh word stirs up anger." (Proverbs 15:1)

Inquire

When our sons were becoming young men, Sandi and I took a class on being a 'Christian Coach'.

Coaches are different than counselors or mentors. Counselors address needs and seek to be a help in the healing process. When I was in pain, I sought the help of a counselor or therapist because I was wounded and needed help. Mentors provide information. When I buy a new computer I need a mentor to show me how to use it. I need someone to teach me and give me knowledge I don't possess.

A coach comes alongside and by skillfully listening and asking questions helps their client to discover what they already know deep inside."The purpose in a man's heart is like deep water, but a man of understanding will draw it out." (Proverbs 20:5) A coach doesn't seek to help you be whole (counselor) or provide new information (mentor), they help you to "work out your own salvation." (Philippians 2:12)

These same skills contribute to good communication. When the speaker has finished expressing what is on their heart, the listener can restate or rephrase what they have heard to see if they have listened well. When Sandi is finished speaking I might sum up what she said and say "Is this what I hear you saying?" My goal is to avoid jumping to conclusions and find out what she has communicated.

I have friends who won't let me complete a sentence, but do it for me. Or they begin to nod and agree when I have not completed my train of thought. They think they know where I am going and are moving faster than I am. This is disconcerting and causes me to stop talking because I am not being heard.

Explore Key Words

Maybe there was some phrase or words which were confusing. Now is the time to have them explained. Perhaps some key words emerged and you can ask the speaker to amplify what they mean. As an example, perhaps the speaker said she felt sad. You could follow up by asking, "What makes you sad?" Here is an example of a conversation I had at an education conference. Tiffany was sitting in the front row and offered to be my volunteer.

Steve: Are you enjoying the education convention?
Tiffany: Yes, very much.
Steve: Why did you come to this conference?
Tiffany: I am looking for encouragement and a math curriculum.
Steve: Have you been encouraged by any of the sessions so far today?
Tiffany: Yes.
Steve: Which one?
Tiffany: I went to a workshop on setting reachable goals for your children and yourself.
Steve: How was this encouraging to you?
Tiffany: I have a tendency to try to do too much and then get discouraged when I am not able to accomplish what I hoped to. She gave specific tips on how to be diligent while also being reasonable.
Steve: I can see this would be encouraging. Could you share one tip?
Tiffany: She said at the end of each day, take one minute and write down five things we were able to

accomplish. At the end of the week, read the lists and you will feel a sense of satisfaction and recognize you did more than you thought.

Steve: This is a great idea. Have you had a chance to look at a math curriculum?

Tiffany: Not yet, but I am planning on going to a workshop on MathUSee after lunch. I heard the author is at the conference and will be presenting.

Steve: Excellent. I think you will come away with some new ideas of how to teach math. You may want to sit where the light from the reflection off his bald head will not be a distraction :-)

As Tiffany is speaking I am listening for key words or expressions I can explore. I focused on "encouragement" and "math curriculum." With this new skill I am acquiring, I find myself conversing with people whom I have never met before and having a meaningful conversation with them. I listen to what they are saying, ask related questions, and then we are both edified. Not only am I learning about them, but they feel valued and heard.

An open-ended question is another possible strategy. Since you have been an understanding and empathetic listener you may have an opportunity to discuss other topics which have not been addressed. Let me ask Tiffany one more question and see what she has to say.

Steve: Is there any other motivation for coming to a conference of this sort you haven't thought of?

Tiffany: Mmmm. Well yes, now that you ask, I like being with a group of people who are all concerned about educating their children.

Steve: Why is this meaningful to you?

Tiffany: Sometimes I feel like I am the only one who is troubled about what my children are learning. Now I find myself in a room with a hundred other parents who share the same concern.

Steve: I hear you. It is easy to feel alone as a parent, and we all need the support of others. Are any of your friends here with you?

Tiffany: Just one, but we saw some ladies in the curriculum hall from our community, and we are planning on meeting tonight for dinner.

Steve: Wonderful. I hope you all go home tomorrow refreshed and reenergized.

Tiffany: I think we will.

Steve: Thanks for being my volunteer.

Tiffany: You're welcome.

Restate

When you have asked questions and explored key words, consider restating what you heard. You might begin by saying, "Is this what I hear you saying?". Another strategy is to say, "Here is what I heard you say. Is my summary accurate?"

When I was attending seminary, I learned there were three sermons preached each Sunday morning; the one the preacher intended to preach, the one the congregation heard, and the one reported in the local newspaper. When the speaker has expressed themselves honestly and clearly to the best of their ability, compare notes to see if you heard the same message they were seeking to communicate.

The Gift of Being Heard

You have spoken clearly, listened carefully, valued the speaker, and clarified what you have heard. You have given a great gift to the one who is speaking. You have heard them. There are so many people who are never given the opportunity to be fully heard and understood. You have devoted time and energy to listening well and are to be commended. Well done.

Prayer

Father teach me how to ask insightful questions and genuinely want to know what is on the heart of the speaker. Help me acquire skills which help me understand and comprehend what is being articulated. In the name of Jesus, amen

CHAPTER 9: PROCESS WHAT YOU HAVE LEARNED

Tips for Processing Together
1 Thoughtfully Respond
2 Lifelong Learners
3 Moccasins
4 Rooted before Walking
5 An Understanding Way
6 When in Doubt, Ask

Up to this point we have been focusing on how we are each to function, whether as a listener or a speaker. After all parties have had a chance to be heard and understood, process what you have learned together.

Thoughtfully Respond

Thoughtfully responding leads to good, open, safe communication. Take time to gather your thoughts, draw a deep breath and pause before graciously responding. "The heart of the righteous ponders how to answer." (Proverbs 15:28)

The opposite of carefully responding is reacting emotionally. When I immediately react in my emotional nature, my remarks are generally abrupt, brusk, and harsh. My tone can be hard. This kind of response will discourage two-way communication and put people in defense mode. Because my eyes have been opened to the awful potential I have to wound the spirit of others, I am much more careful than I have been in the past.

Lifelong Learners

We are still learning and growing in the area of communicating. After two and half years of incredible open and honest communication, Sandi told me something this past spring, and I didn't answer properly. I reacted with a harsh tone and then I walked out of the room. I violated several principles in just a few seconds. About ten minutes later I returned and said, "Honey, I'm sorry. I shouldn't have walked out of the room. I shouldn't have reacted in that tone and I apologize."

Then I beat myself up. In the past I would have been sorry, but I could have received her forgiveness and moved on. This time it was much more difficult because we had been so good for so many years. I was much harder on myself because I expected better of myself, and didn't know how to find grace.

She nipped my self aggrandizement in the bud and said "Steve, I forgive you." She knew I was suffering so she continued, "Stop and look at where we are now. We are so far ahead of where we were three years ago. If this same situation had happened in the past, it might have taken six weeks before we got our hearts back together. I have been told this is a similar pattern in many marriages, fight-distance-reconnect. And now after 30 minutes we are talking, and are already in harmony."

Our pattern of behavior for years had been if we had a disagreement, I would shut down emotionally and there would have been distance in our relationship. Then she would sense the detachment from me and blame herself for the problem asking herself what she should have done differently. She may have even read one of the myriad of marriage books which generally places the blame on the woman for not being more respectful or submissive. We noticed there are very few books calling for the man to shape up; they all seem to lay the onus at the women's doorstep. This is so sad, and wrong.

All of us are going to blow it and react poorly. God's grace is always available. We will always have our sin natures to overcome. When I fall and am convicted, I need to ask forgiveness of the person I offended and then ask God to pardon my sin. "If we confess our sins, he is faithful and just to forgive us our sins and to cleanse us from all unrighteousness." (1 John 1:9)

I also need to remember while conviction is a work of the Spirit of God, condemnation is from our enemy the "accuser of our brothers" (Revelation 12:10) In Christ Jesus there is no condemnation. None. Nada. Zilch. "There is therefore now no condemnation for those who are in Christ Jesus." (Romans 8:1)

Then I need to get back up and not wallow in regret or remorse. "The righteous falls seven times and rises again." (Proverbs 24:16)

Moccasins

My wife did a beautiful job of this recently. She was sharing an observation of a recent Bible study. As she was commenting, one of my theological buttons was triggered. Without going in to specifics, I tried to not react, but in responding, my tone was a little hard. I didn't raise my voice, and I was not ready for battle, but all it took was a little bit of a rough tone on my part and I knew I was being contentious.

Our conversation came to a halt and we did not discuss it further because I had crossed the line. I was not teachable in my spirit. The subject was dropped and we went our separate ways. I felt badly, but she had already gone off to do some errands, so I texted her, "Really sorry for my tone and how I responded to your point." She responded, "I think I know why you feel as you do because I've been walking in your moccasins."

Instead of taking what I said personally, she was taking the mature path and trying to understand the conversation from my perspective. She asked herself, "I wonder why my words affected him this way?" She also said, "I understand how important this is for you, and I get it." She is way ahead of me in this area of not taking information personally and reacting, instead she thoughtfully responds.

Rooted before Walking

The more we are each rooted and grounded in the love of God, the better equipped we are to put ourselves into other people's shoes and imagine what they are thinking and feeling. One of the reasons I took input personally for so long was because I did not comprehend the depth and the scope of the gospel of grace. My identity was not in Christ alone, but I saw myself based on what I did, instead of who I was in Christ.

I have written another book called 'Knowing God's Love' about being cognizant of how much God likes each of His children. I won't rewrite it here, but one of the fruits of knowing you are loved and affectionally liked by God is you can like yourself. When you and your spouse learn to communicate, you will be able to discuss things you have never talked about before. You will become closer as a couple and your relationship will deepen IF, you value yourself as much as God does.

Often the barrier to being more fully known is we have a low image of ourself and do not believe we are valuable. Or we fear if others really knew us as we know ourselves, they would not like us. When we are rooted and grounded in the gospel, and assured by scripture God knows us intimately and still loves us, then we begin to see ourselves as God sees us. His "perfect love" (1 John 4:18) sets us free from fear. His complete knowledge of us, and the fact He created and designed us to be who we are, will transform us. When in doubt please read Psalm 139.

Put your name in these inspired words and drink in the truth. I used my name and changed a few pronouns to give you the flavor. These words are true. You and

I are worthy of being known and loved, because God knows and loves us.

Psalms 139:1 O Lord, you have searched Steve and known Steve!

2 You know when I sit down and when I rise up; you discern my thoughts from afar.

3 You search out my path and my lying down and are acquainted with all Steve's ways.

4 Even before a word is on my tongue, behold, O Lord, you know it altogether.

5 You hem me in, behind and before, and lay your hand upon me.

13 For you formed my inward parts; you knitted me together in my mother's womb.

14 I praise you, for I am fearfully and wonderfully made. Wonderful are your works; my soul knows it very well.

15 My frame was not hidden from you, when I was being made in secret, intricately woven in the depths of the earth.

16 Your eyes saw Steve's unformed substance; in your book were written, every one of them, the days that were formed for Steve, when as yet there was none of them.

17 How precious to me are your thoughts, O God! How vast is the sum of them!

18 If I would count them, they are more than the sand. I awake, and I am still with you.

I would like to reiterate, the more rooted and grounded I am in the love and acceptance of God, the more I accept myself. I feel like I am finally growing up. I am finally becoming comfortable in my own skin. Knowing God loves me for who I am and not for what I do or don't do is wonderfully freeing. Being more secure in my relationship with God frees me up to see life from other people's perspectives.

Jesus knew who He was. If He ever had a doubt, it was dispelled at His baptism and on the Mount of Transfiguration, when His Father boomed from heaven, "This is my beloved Son!" (Matthew 3:17) God's Son was rooted and grounded in the love of His Dad. Because He possessed this knowledge, He could be who He was created to be. He could stand alone against the world, the flesh, and the devil. He could fulfill His calling.

He could also respond and not react. Read through this passage and see how Jesus was the ultimate example of someone who was secure in God:
"For to this you have been called, because Christ also suffered for you, leaving you an example, so that you might follow in His steps. He committed no sin, neither was deceit found in His mouth. When He was reviled, He did not revile in return; when He suffered, He did not threaten, but continued entrusting himself to Him who judges justly." (1 Peter 2:21-23)

When I am reviled, my first thought is to defend myself or react. When I am threatened my tendency is not flight, but fight. But God is helping me and I am making progress. When I see poor driving, instead of being upset, I find myself wondering what that person is going through that is affecting them. When someone is rude or terse, instead of complaining to their superior, I am learning that they may just be having a bad day.

Walking in someone else's shoes begins with my own heart being secured and anchored in the love of God. This is why I spend more time than I ever have, reading the word of God, waiting on God, and immersing myself in truth.

An Understanding Way

Several years ago I read a book called Discovering the Mind of a Woman, by Ken Nair. I have also had a chance to meet Ken and learn more about his story. He was raised, along with a twin brother, in an all-boys orphanage. He then joined an all-male Navy. He had very little contact with women, and when he did get married, God gave them three girls.

One day, his wife drew a line in the sand, and Ken became determined to learn how to understand his wife. The impetus was the verse in 1 Peter 3:7. "Husbands, live with your wives in an understanding way." He reasoned if God called husbands to understand their wives, then they could. One of my chief takeaways in this book was learning to sense the spirit of my wife. We are told men and women are from different planets and men are dunces while women are more spiritual. I don't buy this thinking.

I have observed men are often more in tune with their cars than their wives. I am not a big car aficionado, but I do avoid potholes. When I inadvertently hit one, I wince. It hurts me. There is one stretch of road near our home with several manhole covers. I have talked about this road in a mixed audience and all of the men knew exactly what I meant. We even discussed our different strategies to miss hitting them. All the women in the room on this occasion were oblivious to the need to swerve and avoid the covers.

Maybe men are wired a little differently, but I still believe we can learn to understand our wives better and get in touch with what they are sensing and feeling. Open, honest communication and making an effort to see life through each other's eyes will aid in this process. While I am built to sense a pothole, my wife can feel when I say something which hurts someone. I need her help in learning how to connect with people in a way which is helpful and not hurtful, especially with my children. Her insight and discernment in learning how to speak and hear better is invaluable. We need each other to grow and develop. While I am learning from her, perhaps she needs my help to avoid a front end alignment.

When in Doubt, Ask

To help you reflect on your conversation, you may simply ask each other how you are feeling after you have expressed yourselves. Another way to verbalize this same thought is to ask how this discussion impacted or affected you. Different strategies work for different folks, but when the heart truly wants to know what has been communicated, the tongue will figure out how to articulate the correct question.

Use this time to thank each other for being honest and willing to share feelings. After you have had some discussion, you might want to set a date to follow through on any issues which have been raised.

When you have had a chance to ponder and process together, set aside some time to pray over what has been shared. "Bear one another's burdens, and so fulfill the law of Christ." (Galatians 6:2)

Prayer

"For this reason I bow my knees before the Father, from whom every family in heaven and on earth is named, that according to the riches of his glory he may grant you to be strengthened with power through his Spirit in your inner being, so that Christ may dwell in your hearts through faith—that you, being rooted and grounded in love, may have strength to comprehend with all the saints what is the breadth and length and height and depth, and to know the love of Christ that surpasses knowledge, that you may be filled with all the fullness of God." (Ephesians 3:14–19)

CHAPTER 10: PRACTICE

Communicating as a Couple

Sandi and I have built into our weekly schedule a specific time to communicate. We currently meet Wednesday mornings at 10:00 AM. We call these times chair chats. Often we are seated in two cushy recliners in the sunny part of our house. Our purpose in talking, listening, and communicating together is not to change the way we think but to understand each other. I desire to hear Sandi, understand what she is expressing, value her, while esteeming her more highly than myself. Is this a tall order? Yes. Can it happen naturally? No. I need God's help, which is one of the many reasons I am a Christian. I acknowledge my dependence on His word, His Spirit, and His grace.

Communication between those who are closest to you, particularly family members, can be difficult because you each value and love each other so much. It is often easier to have tough discussions with people who are not as close to you. This doesn't mean you should avoid family meetings, but approach them carefully and find help when you need it.

Since our goal is to truly hear each other, and since we have the potential to wound and hurt each other as well as understand and build each other up like no one else, we want to have our times of heart communication be safe. We want to take whatever steps we need for each person to create an atmosphere conducive to speaking the truth from the heart, and being heard, without being silenced if we have differing opinions. This takes time, practice, and effort. And it is worth it.

Another reason why my wife and I have these scheduled times to talk is because she needs time to think about what she wants to say and how she wants to say it. It is very helpful for her to know there is a specific time when we are going to talk. I on the other hand am more of an extrovert and when I have a question I address it within nanoseconds at the first opportunity. I am not a planner by nature, but I have observed our regular meetings help us address life together in a healthy way.

During the first year we began our chair chats, Sandi would bring note cards to our morning appointments. I silently gulped when I saw the first card with a list of topics, but I learned to turn off the angst and go with the flow. I later learned throughout the week, when items for discussion would come to mind, she would jot the thought down, knowing within a few days we would have an opportunity to discuss it during our chair chat. Being able to count on this time each week is very meaningful to Sandi.

Getting Started

God-honoring, healthy, safe communication does not come naturally to me. I need to practice this new approach and keep at it until it becomes second nature. I also hope by reading thus far, you have begun to see the incredible potential for good and coming from our heart, via our tongue. "Death and life are in the power of the tongue." (Proverbs 18:21) "Out of the abundance the heart, the mouth speaks." (Matthew 12:34)

When my marriage was on the rocks and our family was suffering, I needed to learn how to talk and listen. I desperately sought to learn skills to heal and rebuild the relationships with my family. I learned how to develop a quiet spirit and a teachable heart. I learned how to speak for clarity and listen for understanding. But I am an old dog and learning new tricks takes time and being intentional.

If you would like to apply what you are reading and learning I hope you will set aside time to practice and talk about this information. Most of my experience was in the crucible and the discussions were about deep and painful topics. I wish I had developed some of these strategies years ago, so when life became tough and talking was not easy, I could have applied these skills.

To this end, here are some interesting questions you might consider discussing with your spouse to get the ball rolling. Focus on applying the principles and strategies from the previous nine chapters.

Questions to ask your spouse
1. What are you most thankful for?
2. What is your favorite summer activity?
3. Which season is your favorite and why?
4. Name one person, alive or dead, you would like to meet.

5. Which five books were special to you when you were a youth? When you were a young adult? As an adult?

6. Name three people who have influenced you the most. How did they impact you?

7. Name three favorite movies, when you were a youth When you were a young adult? As an adult?

8. If money were no object, nor was travel, where would you like to spend a day, a week, a month?

9. What does an ideal day look like to you?

10. What experience has stretched you the most?

11. For what are you most thankful?

12. Would you share your favorite childhood memory? As a teen? As a young adult?

13. What was your most painful day as a child? As a teen? As a young adult?

14. What was your favorite job as teen? As a young adult?

15. What would you consider an ideal occupation?

16. What is your most troublesome weakness?

17. What is your greatest strength?

18. If you had to pick three books of the Bible to have with you on an island, which would you choose and why?

19. What is your favorite verse in the Bible? Most meaningful chapter?

20. Can you think of five people from scripture whom you are looking forward to seeing in heaven?

Prayer

May our Lord Jesus Christ himself, and God our Father, who loved us and gave us eternal comfort and good hope through grace, comfort your hearts and establish them in every good work and word. Amen (2 Thessalonians 2:16-17)

CHAPTER 11: AS A FAMILY

As you learn how to communicate more effectively as a couple, consider having the whole family participate in regular communication times. Healthy family communication is built on healthy parents who have learned to have safe conversations. Moms and dads impact their children more by what they model than what they say. Kiddos will observe their parents having healthy interchanges and note the new degree of peace in their relationship. We all yearn for this kind of security in our interactions, especially with those we cherish the most.

As a Family

When you are both feeling comfortable in your ability to converse with each other, consider meeting as a family to pass on your new skills. At the first meeting, think about having the kids come up with their own rules or code. This could be an interesting time as you solicit their input. They may say, "Nobody is allowed to interrupt me." Or, "Please don't holler when someone is talking." Kids are very discerning and this could be a wonderful opportunity to hear what they value.

A little piece of advice for parents before you first meet as a family: Let's assume you haven't always been the best listener in the past and have wounded some or all of the children, like most parents. Your family has summoned their courage and you are beginning the first session. You have come up with a list of rules; remember you can add to or tweak them whenever you need to, since it is your list.

Taking the Plunge

I am going to predict one of your kiddos will test the waters to see if this is going to be a safe experience. This brave child may toss out a verbal hand grenade to see how the parents are going to respond. If he were in my family, he may say, "I don't think you should use blocks to teach math." This is sure to push my button, and he is fully aware of how I will react, which is why he chose this comment. Children need to see whether I will respond or react. How I reply, and my tone, will be a signal for the rest of the family.

If I dismiss it out of hand, or react angrily, or say something like, "Well you better be careful what you say mister, because those blocks pay for your food!" Then everyone will withdraw. But if I thoughtfully respond and say, "Why do you think blocks are not effective?" or "What do you think is a good way to teach math?" and truly listen with respect to his response, I am creating a safe place where other less explosive topics may be addressed.

Maybe the next brave child will say, "I want to get a tattoo." Everyone holds their breath, for this might be an extreme test for you. If your family is anything like ours, they know what I like and dislike. Maybe you have an aversion to tattoos. This is why she chose this topic.

Are you going to say, "What color tattoo would you like to have?" or "Absolutely not!" You have every right to your own opinion of tattoos, so do your children. The object of a family discussion is to not agree or disagree but to understand. An honest answer may be, "Well, I need a minute to take a deep breath and think about what you have said. You all know I am not a fan of tattoos, but I would like to hear what you think." You are being honest, you are processing your feelings aloud, and you are still at the table, and not issuing ultimatums." In my mind, what transpires after this point is unimportant, because you have modeled so well the essence of honest, open discourse in the sharing of yourself and what you are feeling, while valuing and striving to hear your child.

When your family sees you are serious about really listening to them, and they feel safe, beautiful times of connecting a a heart level will happen. Give your family time to warm up to the idea while you continue to win their trust. It may take years to establish this kind of confidence. Hang in there.

Breathe

Just as we discussed in the earlier section on ultimatums and time-outs, we all will experience times when we need time and perhaps space to respond thoughtfully and not react emotionally. When families gather together, children may confront their parents with their hypocrisy or inconsistency.

Instead of pulling the authority card and telling your kids to back off when you feel attacked or you sense an angry retort forming in your breast, take a deep breath. Remain open and present, perhaps call a time-out and give yourself time to process what you are feeling. You are human. You have emotions. So do your children and spouse. Be real. Acknowledge you are struggling to process what has been said and respond in a positive manner. Your example will have a tremendous impact on the whole family.

Have Patience and Seek Feedback

After 2012, the hardest and best year of my life, I took my three older sons out to lunch and made myself available to them. I said, "I know you have forgiven me for things I have said and done, but I am your dad and I know I have wounded you. Whenever you're ready to tell me the ways in which I have wounded you or feel the need to confront me, I'm willing to hear what you have to say. If you need to vent, or are seeking closure, I'm willing to meet with you, you and your therapist, you and your wife, or you and your church. I want you to be whole, and I'm dead serious about this."

One of my boys got in the car immediately after lunch and began to talk. Another began dropping little pieces of information over the next few few months to see how I would respond. But almost two years passed before we made an appointment to talk one-on-one. The two of us met in his home where he read me a letter he had composed several months earlier. We talked our hearts out for almost three hours. It was hard and painful but a major breakthrough occurred.

I heard what he had faced growing up with me as his Dad, what I had done right, and what I had done wrong, the whole package. I got to hear it, but it took several years for him to believe I was serious and earn his trust. A few months later I asked him, "how are you doing?" He said, "Pop, I'm good because I have nothing I'm holding back from you. I have told you everything."

It takes awhile to rebuild the trust before you can experience open, honest, safe communication. Be patient and remember principle number one, "Pursue a heart trusting and resting in the love of your heavenly Dad first." My wife and kids and I have never been in a better place than we are right now. We had to go through hell to get here, and I had to work through a lot of my own painful stuff, but it was so worth the effort.

Maintain the prime objective

Encourage each member of your home to have personal times of waiting on God and developing a settled, soft heart which is in a place of peace. Read the word of God together as a family and pray together before each meeting. Maintain the prime directive which is to communicate for clarity and not to convince or change the way someone thinks.

Teach the skills necessary for a speaker and a listener. Learn to apply your unique code of conduct you have put together as a family team. Learn how to ask good questions. Practice restating what you have heard for clarity. Listen for words you can ask the speaker to expand on so you can explore more of what she is thinking.

Practice as a family just as you have practiced as a couple. Save the potentially harmful and explosive topics until you are each comfortable with easier subjects. Without pressuring each person to participate, conduct several conversations by asking someone to go first and possess the pen. A starter query might be: "What is your favorite family activity?" Then each person can apply their skills as a listener to maintain eye contact, turn off electronics, ask questions for clarification, and affirm the speaker.

I quizzed a few children during a recent workshop and asked what their favorite thing to do was. One little boy said, "I just like to hang out with Dad and do whatever he is doing." I hope his dad heard him, because I almost cried on the spot. Children want to be near us, but sometimes we don't know what is going on in their hearts until we give them a chance to speak.

I met one family which sets time aside every Sunday afternoon for one-on-one discussions with each of their children. While the kids are lazing around, Mom and dad are in another room. They call in each child, one at a time, to give them a chance to talk and ask questions. While there is wonderful potential discoursing about life as a group, it is also important to give each person individual time as well. I met some of the children in this family, and they seemed content and confident.

Relationships are built with positive healthy two-way communication. My relationship with God sets the tone for my relationship with my wife and subsequently my sons. When I am abiding in the steadfast unchanging love of my Dad, then I am able to have deep and meaningful times with my wife and sons. Bottom line, treat each other as you want to be treated.

Remember, Family Matters

"At the same time, saith the LORD, will I be the God of all the families of Israel, and they shall be my people." (Jeremiah 31:1 KJV)

At one point in our family discussions I discovered the pain I had been causing my sons. I was distraught and devastated. I surmised the best thing to do would be to walk away and remove myself from the equation. I was unable to speak without breaking into tears, so I wrote on a piece of paper, "I'll hand the business over to you and walk away." Do you know what my sons did? They passed the paper back and said, "We don't want your business, we want you."

We are each a part of a family. Our kids want us. We want them. Husbands and wives want each other. Learning how to communicate in a safe edifying manner takes work. But when we make the effort, the results are wonderful. Our family no longer needs a consultant to oversee and facilitate our discussions. We are learning how to address elephants which have been in the room for a generation, with success.

I hope these principles which have helped our family will be a help to your family as well.

Prayer

"May the God of peace who brought again from the dead our Lord Jesus, the great shepherd of the sheep, by the blood of the eternal covenant, equip you with everything good that you may do his will, working in us that which is pleasing in his sight, through Jesus Christ, to whom be glory forever and ever. Amen." (Hebrews 13:20–21)

CHAPTER 12:
IN CASE OF AN
EMERGENCY CALL
FOR HELP

When I was taking the class on Family Therapy, Steve, the professor, mentioned he had been meeting with some couples for over a decade. I was surprised to hear this because I surmised when husbands and wives learned these principles and applied them they would outgrow the need to continue seeing a therapist. I asked for more information and he said a particular couple would schedule an appointment whenever they had to tackle difficult issues or make decisions. They needed him to to be there as a facilitator and third party.

When Sandi and I were struggling in our marriage, we enlisted the help of Steve to meet with us as a couple and help us learn to speak and hear each other. Sandi and I continue to meet for our weekly chair chats and we have been a part of a small group in which we learn and grow together. Life is a journey.

Our family benefitted from a consultant who was both qualified in setting up a corporation as well as counseling families. Mike became a personal friend and his counsel, expertise, and general demeanor were invaluable to us at a critical juncture for our family and business.

Since those initial years, we have had a few family concerns we believed would benefit from having one or both of these men at the table and have reenlisted their services. For the most part though, we are able to use the skills we have learned to work through life on our own.

If you are in a difficult place, pray about finding someone to sit at the table so you may use their expertise and experience to help your family. I do not believe there is anything more important than my relationship with God, my wife, and my sons. I pay fees for lawyers, accountants, financial experts, mechanics, doctors, dentists, trainers, and lawn care. Should I not also invest in finding help in this most important arena?

If you begin to look for a third party, ask friends for referrals, pray, and do your homework. My next statements may surprise you. I am a believer in Jesus. Both Mike and Steve are believers. But we hired them based on their track record and referrals more than their faith. I would rather have a qualified accountant who was diligent and honest regardless of his profession of faith, rather than someone who was born again but incompetent.

I also know there are Christian mediation services available, but I have not had good experiences with them, nor have my associates. A good heart is great, but it cannot replace experience and training. I know sad stories of well meaning men and women in ministry who tried to counsel folks and did more harm than good.

My advice is if you need help as an individual, a couple, or a family, go get the help you need. Do not hesitate. I vowed I would never see a "shrink," but when I was desperate, it was just such a person who helped me, my marriage, and my family immeasurably. Look for the right person. The first counselor I went to was not a good fit and I went elsewhere. I looked until I found someone who could help. God will provide. "Ask and it will be given you. Seek and you will find." (Luke 11:9) You would not be reading this book if I had not humbled myself and asked for help.

CHAPTER 13:
THE POWER TO BLESS

The first chapter in this book was the power of the tongue. "From the same mouth come blessing and cursing." James 3:10. I've also observed family members, and those who are closest to us, have the most potential to build up or to wound with words. Since we began with recognizing the potential to curse, I would like to close the book recognizing the power to bless.

At a men's conference, I had the privilege of witnessing a blessing. The father, who had MS and was unable to stand, blessed his son and bride at their wedding. I was amazed and inspired to hear the scriptural truths pour forth from this elderly saint's heart and mind as he blessed these two newlyweds. Without a script, this godly man spoke truth over, and into, the lives of this devoted young couple for at least five minutes.

I felt as if I was on holy ground as I witnessed this powerful event which was videotaped fifteen years earlier. The experience was so sacred and moving I had trouble processing what I had just witnessed. The words and evident love and affection between father and son impacted me at a deep level. Even now I am still trying to assimilate what I observed.

A little background: This grainy family wedding video was being shown to a group of ministry leaders at a conference where we were seeking to find ways by which we could teach and encourage fathers. As one man succinctly stated, all of the current social ills of our society stem from fatherlessness. After two days of deliberating on the current situation in our country, we were now observing the antidote, an anointed example of a godly father affirming and blessing his son and his new daughter-in-law.

The father, who was the vehicle for this heavenly benediction, had not been raised in a godly Christian home. He desperately wanted his children to have every spiritual advantage he had not received. To that end, he read every book he could procure on raising godly children, including *The Blessing* by John Trent and Gary Smalley.

When the video concluded, the son, who was the beneficiary of those inspired words, stood and addressed us with words of comfort and hope. Many of us were wishing we had received a similar blessing from our father, and he comforted us by pointing us to the word of God. In Ephesians 1:3 the Spirit informs us "the God and Father of our Lord Jesus Christ, ... has blessed us in Christ with every spiritual blessing." While we may not have received a blessing from our earthly dads, in Christ, we have been given, "every spiritual blessing".

Then this man, who I will identify later, imparted a vision and hope for the next generation, as he told us what it was like being the recipient of such an anointed blessing. He said many children live FOR the blessing of their father, while he lives FROM the blessing of his father. I hope you will mediate on the distinction.

Many of my friends and I are looking for approval and acceptance from our dad. I could tell you many examples but one sticks out to me. I was watching the U.S. Open on Father's Day with my brother and my dad. Ken Venturi, who had won one major championships, bared his soul and told how he longed to have his father say "Well done, son". For him, golf had been the vehicle to earn this praise. But regardless of how well he did, his father never affirmed him. One day, when he was facing surgery on his hand which might prohibit him from ever playing golf again, he sought out his dad. He explained the gravity of the situation and asked his advice. His father listened and then told him "Regardless of what happens, you have always been number one in my book." Those simple words changed his life.

I am one of many who would dearly love to have a written or verbal blessing from my earthly dad. He did the best he could, with the resources he had, and I rise up and honor his memory. But deep down I crave the affirmation only a dad can bequeath. In the past few years, the Spirit of God has satisfied this longing by making me know in my heart I am an adopted son of my Heavenly Father.

Now I am a father, and it is my earnest hope and desire my sons will experience life not looking FOR my blessing, but living FROM my blessing. You and I are living in troubled times, but also wonderful times. For the Spirit of God is turning the hearts of fathers to their children, children's hearts to their father, and all of our hearts to our Heavenly Dad.

In case you are wondering, the man who received the blessing was Stephen Kendrick. He related his frail father had also pronounced similar blessings at his brother's weddings. Part of the blessing was his sons would be fruitful in reaching thousands with the gospel. If the name is not familiar, these Kendrick brothers have produced several inspiring movies pointing thousands of people to Christ, including Fireproof, Courageous, and War Room.

Words matter. The tongue has the power to curse and bless. If you would like to bless your own children I would suggest the priestly blessing, "The LORD bless you and keep you; the LORD make his face to shine upon you and be gracious to you; the LORD lift up his countenance upon you and give you peace." (Numbers 6:24–26) I added several more benedictions in the Appendix of scriptures for Chapter 13.

Prayer

May the God of peace himself sanctify you completely, and may your whole spi-rit and soul and body be kept blameless at the coming of our Lord Jesus Christ. He who calls you is faithful; he will surely do it. (1 Thessalonians 5:23–24)

CHAPTER 14: CONCLUSION

You have read the book and heard my heart. Without summarizing all you have read, allow me to hit a few high points to review.

Words are powerful in and of themselves. When they are spoken by people whom we love and respect, their influence is magnified. No one has the potential to build up and encourage me like my wife and sons. Conversely no one can hurt or tear down my wife and sons like me.

Good words and healthy listening skills do not come from my tongue but my heart. When my heart is marinating in the grace and kindness of God, my mouth will be a source of comfort and encouragement. A quiet spirit and a peaceful heart are the prerequisites for safe and profitable discourse.

My own life was transformed recently in grasping and comprehending the gospel in new and deeper ways. I have become reacquainted with the love of God. I know I am an adopted child of God, who not only loves me, but genuinely likes me. My Dad and I have a wonderful relationship. I know God is for me.

The assurance I am loved and liked has overflowed and impacted my relationship with my wife and sons. The more I immerse myself in the love of God and seek to be rooted and grounded in Christ alone, the better able I am to speak honestly and openly and listen compassionately.

Loving relationships do not just happen. They are built through verbal and nonverbal communication. I need to continue to practice these skills to make them second nature. While some of them are common sense, others are not and require sustained effort and practice. My wife and I are now into our third year of our regularly scheduled chair chats.

I have a vision, a dream if you will, of an ideal family. It is where every person is rooted and grounded in God, and thus enabled to love each other as God has, and is, loving them. I have a hope Christian homes will be safe places where every family member is free to speak and be heard regardless of the content of his or her speech. As a result of every person's connection with God and the acceptance and support of their family, they will each be built up and encouraged to be who God designed them to be.

When family after family is transformed through applying these principles, I envision robust growing churches, and healthy flourishing cities and towns. For the family, created and designed by God, is the foundation for our communities of faith and service.

Prayer

"May the Lord direct our hearts to the love of God and to the steadfastness of Christ. And may the words of our mouth and the meditation of our heart be acceptable in your sight, O Lord, our rock and our redeemer." (Adapted from 2 Thessalonians 3:5 and Psalms 19:14.)

APPENDIX

A list of scriptures in each chapter as well as additional passages on communication.

Chapter 1 The Power of the Tongue
Proverbs 18:21 Death and life are in the power of the tongue,

Proverbs 15:4 A gentle tongue is a tree of life, but perverseness in it breaks the spirit.

James 3:9 With it we bless our Lord and Father, and with it we curse people who are made in the likeness of God. 10 From the same mouth come blessing and cursing. My brothers, these things ought not to be so.

Isaiah 50:4 The Lord GOD has given me the tongue of those who are taught, that I may know how to sustain with a word him who is weary.

Chapter 2, The Heart and Tongue are Connected
Luke 12:34 Where your treasure is, there will your heart be also.

Matthew 12:34 Out of the abundance of the heart the mouth speaks.

James 4:1 What causes quarrels and what causes fights among you? Is it not this, that your passions are at war within you?

Matthew 15:17-20 Do you not see that whatever goes into the mouth passes into the stomach and is expelled? But what comes out of the mouth proceeds from the heart, and this defiles a person. For out of the heart come evil thoughts, murder, adultery, sexual immorality, theft, false witness, slander. These are what defile a person.

Galatians 5:15-24 If you bite and devour one another, watch out that you are not consumed by one another. But I say, walk by the Spirit, and you will not gratify the desires of the flesh. For the desires of the flesh are against the Spirit, and the desires of the Spirit are against the flesh, for these are opposed to each other, to keep you from doing the things you want to do. But if you are led by the Spirit, you are not under the law. Now the works of the flesh are evident: sexual immorality, impurity, sensuality, idolatry, sorcery, enmity, strife, jealousy, fits of anger, rivalries, dissensions, divisions, envy, drunkenness, orgies, and things like these. I warn you, as I warned you before, that those who do such things will not inherit the kingdom of God. But the fruit of the Spirit is love, joy, peace, patience, kindness, goodness, faithfulness, gentleness, self-control; against such things there is no law. And those who belong to Christ Jesus have crucified the flesh with its passions and desires."

Matthew 7:3 Why do you see the speck that is in your brother's eye, but do not notice the log that is in your own eye?

Matthew 7:4-5 Let me take the speck out of your eye, when there is the log in your own eye? You hypocrite, first take the log out of your own eye, and then you will see clearly to take the speck out of your brother's eye.

Luke 6:45 The good person out of the good treasure of his heart produces good, and the evil person out of his evil treasure produces evil, for out of the abundance of the heart his mouth speaks.

Psalms 51:10 Create in me a clean heart, O God, and renew a right spirit within me.

Psalm 19:14 Let the words of my mouth and the meditation of my heart Be acceptable in thy sight, O the LORD, my rock, and my redeemer.

Chapter 3 A Quiet Heart
Romans 8:15 You did not receive the spirit of slavery to fall back into fear, but you have received the Spirit of adoption as sons, by whom we cry, "Abba! Father!"

Galatians 4:6 Because you are sons, God has sent the Spirit of his Son into our hearts, crying, "Abba! Father!"

1 John 4:19 We love because he first loved us.

Romans 5:8 God shows his love for us in that while we were still sinners, Christ died for us.

Luke 15:20 And the father saw him afar off. The father with compassion ran down the street and embraced him.

1 John 4:16 God is love.

1 John 1:5 God is light, and in Him is no darkness at all.

Hebrews 13:8 He is the same yesterday, today, and forever.

Ephesians 3:14-19 For this reason I bow my knees before the Father, from whom every family in heaven and on earth is named, that according to the riches of his glory he may grant you to be strengthened with power through his Spirit in your inner being, so that Christ may dwell in your hearts through faith—that you, being rooted and grounded in love, may have strength to comprehend with all the saints what is the breadth and length and height and depth, and to know the love of Christ that surpasses knowledge, that you may be filled with all the fullness of God.

Romans 5:5 God's love has been poured into our hearts through the Holy Spirit who has been given to us.

2 Thessalonians 3:5 May the Lord direct your hearts to the love of God and to the steadfastness of Christ.

Chapter 4 Esteem One Another Highly
Philippians 2:3-8 Do nothing from selfish ambition or

conceit, but in humility count others more significant than yourselves. Let each of you look not only to his own interests, but also to the interests of others. Have this mind among yourselves, which is yours in Christ Jesus, who, though He was in the form of God, did not count equality with God a thing to be grasped, but emptied Himself, by taking the form of a servant, being born in the likeness of men. And being found in human form, He humbled himself by becoming obedient to the point of death, even death on a cross.

Proverbs 23:7 For as he thinks within himself, so he is. NASB

Matthew 20:26. You know that the rulers of the Gentiles lord it over them, and their great ones exercise authority over them. It shall not be so among you. But whoever would be great among you must be your servant.

John 13:3-5 Jesus, knowing that the Father had given all things into His hands, and that He had come from God and was going back to God, rose from supper. He laid aside His outer garments, and taking a towel, tied it around His waist. Then He poured water into a basin and began to wash the disciples' feet and to wipe them with the towel that was wrapped around Him."

John 13:12-15 Do you understand what I have done to you? You call me Teacher and Lord, and you are right, for so I am. If I then, your Lord and Teacher, have washed your feet, you also ought to wash one another's feet. For I have given you an example, that you also should do just as I have done to you.

2 Corinthians 13:10 For this reason I write these things while I am away from you, that when I come I may not have to be severe in my use of the authority that the Lord has given me for building up and not for tearing down.

Romans 12:3 By the grace given to me I say to everyone among you not to think of himself more highly than he ought to think, but to think with sober judgment, each according to the measure of faith that God has assigned.

Chapter 5 Create a Safe Place with Ground Rules
2 Corinthians 13:10 For this reason I write these things while I am away from you, that when I come I may not have to be severe in my use of the authority that the Lord has given me for building up and not for tearing down.

Matthew 12:18–20 Behold, my servant whom I have chosen, my beloved with whom my soul is well pleased. I will put my Spirit upon Him, and He will proclaim justice to the Gentiles. He will not quarrel or cry aloud, nor will anyone hear His voice in the streets; a bruised reed He will not break, and a smoldering wick He will not quench.

Matthew 11:28-30 "Come to me, all who labor and are heavy laden, and I will give you rest. Take my yoke upon you, and learn from me, for I am gentle and lowly in heart, and you will find rest for your souls. For my yoke is easy, and my burden is light."

John 15:9 As the Father has loved me, so have I loved you. Abide in my love.

John 15:12 "This is my commandment, that you love one another as I have loved you.

1 Corinthians 13:4-7 Love is patient and kind; love does not envy or boast; it is not arrogant or rude. It does not insist on its own way; it is not irritable or resentful; it does not rejoice at wrongdoing, but rejoices with the truth. Love bears all things, believes all things, hopes all things, endures all things.

Replacing Love with Jesus
1 Corinthians 13:4-7 Jesus is patient and kind; Jesus does not envy or boast; He is not arrogant or rude. He does not insist on its own way; He is not irritable or resentful; He does not rejoice at wrongdoing, but rejoices with the truth. Jesus bears all things, believes all things, hopes all things, endures all things.

Romans 14:5 Each one should be fully convinced in his own mind.

Romans 14:19 So then let us pursue what makes for peace and for mutual upbuilding.

Chapter 6 Speak the Truth With Love
Ephesians 4:15 Speaking the truth in love, we are to grow up in every way into him who is the head, into Christ,

James 1:26 If you claim to be religious but don't control your tongue, you are fooling yourself."

Psalms 85:10 Mercy and truth are met together; righteousness and peace have kissed each other. ASV

John 1:17 For the law was given through Moses; grace and truth came through Jesus Christ. grace and truth came through Jesus Christ.

Psalm 6:3 My soul also is greatly troubled. But you, O Lord— how long?

Psalm 6:6-7 I am weary with my moaning; every night I flood my bed with tears; I drench my couch with my weeping. My eye wastes away because of grief; it grows weak because of all my foes.

Psalm 13:1-2 How long, O Lord? Will you forget me forever? How long will you hide your face from me? How long must I take counsel in my soul and have sorrow in my heart all the day?

Acts 17:11 Now these were more noble than those in Thessalonica, in that they received the word with all readiness of the mind, examining the scriptures daily, whether these things were so.

1 Peter 3:15 Always being prepared to make a defense to anyone who asks you for a reason for the hope that is in you; yet do it with gentleness and respect.

Matthew 5:37 Let what you say be simply 'Yes' or 'No'; anything more than this comes from evil.

Psalms 141:3 Set a guard, O LORD, over my mouth; keep watch over the door of my lips!

Colossians 4:6 Let your speech always be gracious, seasoned with salt, so that you may know how you ought to answer each person.

Chapter 7 Be Quick to Hear and Slow to Speak
James 1:19 Know this, my beloved brothers: let every person be quick to hear, slow to speak

Ephesians 3:16-19 According to the riches of his glory he may grant you to be strengthened with power through his Spirit in your inner being, so that Christ may dwell in your hearts through faith—that you, being rooted and grounded in love may have strength to comprehend with all the saints what is the breadth and length and height and depth, and to know the love of Christ that surpasses knowledge, that you may be filled with all the fullness of God.

Proverbs 16:32 Whoever is slow to anger is better than the mighty, and he who rules his spirit than he who takes a city.

Psalms 139:14 I praise you, for I am fearfully and wonderfully made. Wonderful are your works; my soul knows it very well.

2 Corinthians 4:7 We have this treasure in jars of clay, to show that the surpassing power belongs to God and not to us.

Chapter 8 Ask and Explore

James 4:2 You do not have, because you do not ask.

Galatians 5:23 gentleness, self-control; against such things there is no law.

Proverbs 15:1 A soft answer turns away wrath, but a harsh word stirs up anger.

Proverbs 20:5 The purpose in a man's heart is like deep water, but a man of under-standing will draw it out.

Philippians 2:12 Therefore, my beloved, as you have always obeyed, so now, not only as in my presence but much more in my absence, work out your own salvation with fear and trembling,

Joshua 22:10 And when they came to the region of the Jordan that is in the land of Canaan, the people of Reuben and the people of Gad and the half-tribe of Manasseh built there an altar by the Jordan, an altar of imposing size. 11 And the people of Is-rael heard it said, "Behold, the people of Reuben and the people of Gad and the half-tribe of Manasseh have built the altar at the frontier of the land of Canaan, in the re-gion about the Jordan, on the side that belongs to the people of Israel." 12 And when the people of Israel heard of it, the whole assembly of the people of Israel gathered at Shiloh to make war against them.

Joshua 22:15 they said to them, 16 "Thus says the whole congregation of the LORD, 'What is this breach of faith that you have committed against the God of Israel in turning away this day from following the LORD by building yourselves an altar this day in rebellion against the LORD?

Joshua 22:21 Then the people of Reuben, the people of Gad, and the half-tribe of Manasseh said in answer to the heads of the families of Israel, 22 "The Mighty One, God, the LORD! The Mighty One, God, the LORD! He knows; and let Israel itself know!

Joshua 22:30 When Phinehas the priest and the chiefs of the congregation, the heads of the families of Israel who were with him, heard the words that the people of Reu-ben and the people of Gad and the people of Manasseh spoke, it was good in their eyes.

Chapter 9 Process What You Have Learned
Proverbs 15:28 The heart of the righteous ponders how to answer,

1 John 1:9 If we confess our sins, he is faithful and just to forgive us our sins and to cleanse us from all unrighteousness.

Revelation 12:10 And I heard a loud voice in heaven, saying, "Now the salvation and the power and the kingdom of our God and the authority of his Christ have come, for the accuser of our brothers has been thrown down, who accuses them day and night before our God.

Romans 8:1 There is therefore now no condemnation for those who are in Christ Jesus.

Proverbs 24:16 The righteous falls seven times and rises again.

1 John 4:18 There is no fear in love, but perfect love casts out fear. For fear has to do with punishment, and whoever fears has not been perfected in love.

Psalms 139:1 O LORD, you have searched me and known me!

2 You know when I sit down and when I rise up; you discern my thoughts from afar.

3 You search out my path and my lying down and are acquainted with all my ways.

4 Even before a word is on my tongue, behold, O LORD, you know it altogether.

5 You hem me in, behind and before, and lay your hand upon me.

6 Such knowledge is too wonderful for me; it is high; I cannot attain it.

7 Where shall I go from your Spirit? Or where shall I flee from your presence?

8 If I ascend to heaven, you are there! If I make my bed in Sheol, you are there!

9 If I take the wings of the morning and dwell in the uttermost parts of the sea,

10 even there your hand shall lead me, and your right hand shall hold me.

11 If I say, "Surely the darkness shall cover me, and the light about me be night,"

12 even the darkness is not dark to you; the night is bright as the day, for darkness is as light with you.

13 For you formed my inward parts; you knitted me together in my mother's womb.

14 I praise you, for I am fearfully and wonderfully made. Wonderful are your works; my soul knows it very well.

15 My frame was not hidden from you, when I was being made in secret, intricately woven in the depths of the earth.

16 Your eyes saw my unformed substance; in your book were written, every one of them, the days that were formed for me, when as yet there was none of them.

17 How precious to me are your thoughts, O God! How vast is the sum of them!

18 If I would count them, they are more than the sand. I awake, and I am still with you.

Matthew 3:17 This is my beloved Son!

1 Peter 2:21-23 For to this you have been called, because Christ also suffered for you, leaving you an example, so that you might follow in his steps. He committed no sin, neither was deceit found in his

mouth. When he was reviled, he did not revile in return; when he suffered, he did not threaten, but continued entrusting himself to Him who judges justly.

1 Peter 3:7 Husbands, live with your wives in an understanding way

Galatians 6:2 Bear one another's burdens, and so fulfill the law of Christ.

Ephesians 3:14-19 For this reason I bow my knees before the Father, from whom every family in heaven and on earth is named, that according to the riches of his glory he may grant you to be strengthened with power through his Spirit in your inner being, so that Christ may dwell in your hearts through faith—that you, being rooted and grounded in love, may have strength to comprehend with all the saints what is the breadth and length and height and depth, and to know the love of Christ that surpasses knowledge, that you may be filled with all the fullness of God.

Chapter 10 Practice
Proverbs 18:21 Death and life are in the power of the tongue.

Matthew 12:34 Out of the abundance our heart, our mouth speaks.

2 Thessalonians 2:16-17 May our Lord Jesus Christ himself, and God our Father, who loved us and gave

us eternal comfort and good hope through grace, comfort your he-arts and establish them in every good work and word. Amen

Chapter 11 As a Family
Jeremiah 31:1 At the same time, saith the LORD, will I be the God of all the families of Israel, and they shall be my people. KJV

Hebrews 13:20-21 May the God of peace who brought again from the dead our Lord Jesus, the great shepherd of the sheep, by the blood of the eternal covenant, equip you with everything good that you may do his will, working in us that which is pleasing in his sight, through Jesus Christ, to whom be glory forever and ever. Amen.

Chapter 12 In Case of an Emergency Call for Help
Luke 11:9 And I tell you, ask, and it will be given to you; seek, and you will find; knock, and it will be opened to you. 10 For everyone who asks receives, and the one who seeks finds, and to the one who knocks it will be opened.

Chapter 13 The Power to Bless
James 3:10 From the same mouth come blessing and cursing.

Ephesians 1:3 Blessed be the God and Father of our Lord Jesus Christ, who has blessed us in Christ with every spiritual blessing in the heavenly places,

Numbers 6:24 The LORD bless you and keep you; 25 the LORD make his face to shine upon you and be gracious to you; 26 the LORD lift up his countenance upon you and give you peace. 27 "So shall they put my name upon the people of Israel, and I will bless them."

1 Thessalonians 5:23-24 May the God of peace himself sanctify you completely, and may your whole spirit and soul and body be kept blameless at the coming of our Lord Jesus Christ. He who calls you is faithful; he will surely do it.

Additional Benedictions for your Family
2 Thessalonians 2:16-17 May our Lord Jesus Christ himself, and God our Father, who loved us and gave us eternal comfort and good hope through grace, comfort your he-arts and establish them in every good work and word.

2 Thessalonians 3:5 May the Lord direct your hearts into the love of God and into the steadfastness of Christ.

Philippians 4:23 The grace of the Lord Jesus Christ be with your spirit

Hebrews 13:20-21 May the God of peace who brought again from the dead our Lord Jesus, the great shepherd of the sheep, by the blood of the eternal covenant, equip you with everything good that you may do his will, working in us that which is plea-sing in his sight, through Jesus Christ, to whom be glory forever and ever. Amen.

2 Peter 1:2 May grace and peace be multiplied to you in the knowledge of God and of Jesus our Lord.

Chapter 14 Conclusion

2 Thessalonians 3:5 May the Lord direct our hearts to the love of God and to the steadfastness of Christ.

Psalms 19:14 May the words of our mouth and the meditation of our heart be acceptable in your sight, O Lord, our rock and our redeemer."

Additional Scriptures on Communication

Self Control

Job 32:18 For I am full of words; the spirit within me constrains me.

Psalms 141:3 Set a guard, O LORD, over my mouth; keep watch over the door of my lips!

Proverbs 10:19 When words are many, transgression is not lacking, but whoever restrains his lips is prudent.

Proverbs 13:3 Whoever guards his mouth preserves his life; he who opens wide his lips comes to ruin.

Proverbs 15:23 To make an apt answer is a joy to a man, and a word in season, how good it is!

Proverbs 15:28 The heart of the righteous ponders how to answer, but the mouth of the wicked pours out evil things.

Proverbs 16:32 Whoever is slow to anger is better than the mighty, and he who rules his spirit than he who takes a city.

Proverbs 17:27 Whoever restrains his words has knowledge, and he who has a cool spirit is a man of understanding.

Proverbs 21:23 Whoever keeps his mouth and his tongue keeps himself out of trouble.

Proverbs 29:11 A fool gives full vent to his spirit, but a wise man quietly holds it back.

Proverbs 29:20 Do you see a man who is hasty in his words? There is more hope for a fool than for him.

James 1:26 If anyone thinks he is religious and does not bridle his tongue but deceives his heart, this person's religion is worthless.

James 3:2 For we all stumble in many ways. And if anyone does not stumble in what he says, he is a perfect man, able also to bridle his whole body.

James 3:17 But the wisdom from above is first pure, then peaceable, gentle, open to reason, full of mercy and good fruits, impartial and sincere. ESV

James 3:17 But the wisdom from above is first of all pure. It is also peace loving, gentle at all times, and willing to yield to others. It is full of mercy and good deeds. It shows no favoritism and is always sincere. NLT

1 Peter 3:10 For "Whoever desires to love life and see good days, let him keep his tongue from evil and his lips from speaking deceit;

Power of Words
Proverbs 15:4 A gentle tongue is a tree of life, but perverseness in it breaks the spirit.

Proverbs 16:24 Gracious(Pleasant) words are like a honeycomb, sweetness to the soul and health to the body.

Proverbs 17:22 A joyful heart is good medicine, but a crushed spirit dries up the bones.

Proverbs 18:21 Death and life are in the power of the tongue,

Proverbs 25:15 With patience a ruler may be persuaded, and a soft tongue will break a bone.

Proverbs 31:26 She opens her mouth with wisdom; And the law of kindness is on her tongue.

Isaiah 50:4 The Lord GOD has given me the tongue of those who are taught, that I may know how to sustain with a word him who is weary. Morning by morning he awakens; he awakens my ear to hear as those who are taught.

Colossians 4:6 Let your speech always be gracious, seasoned with salt, so that you may know how you ought to answer each person.

James 3:1 Not many of you should become teachers, my brothers, for you know that we who teach will be judged with greater strictness. 2 For we all stumble in many ways. And if anyone does not stumble in what he says, he is a perfect man, able also to bridle his whole body. 3 If we put bits into the mouths of horses so that they obey us, we guide their whole bodies as well. 4 Look at the ships also: though they are so large and are driven by strong winds, they are guided by a very small rudder wherever the will of the pilot directs. 5 So also the tongue is a small member, yet it boasts of great things. How great a forest is set ablaze by such a small fire! 6 And the tongue is a fire, a world of unrighteousness. The tongue is set among our members, staining the whole body, setting on fire the entire course of life, and set on fire by hell. 7 For every kind of beast and bird, of reptile and sea creature, can be tamed and has been tamed by mankind, 8 but no human being can tame the tongue. It is a restless evil, full of deadly poison. 9 With it we bless our Lord and Father, and with it we curse people who are made in the likeness of God. 10 From the same mouth come blessing and cursing. My brothers, these things ought not to be so.

1 Peter 3:15 but in your hearts honor Christ the Lord as holy, always being prepared to make a defense to anyone who asks you for a reason for the hope that is in you; yet do it with gentleness and respect,

Miscellaneous Proverbs and Communication
Proverbs 6:16-17 There are six things that the LORD hates, seven that are an abomination to him: haughty eyes, a lying tongue, and hands that shed innocent blood,

Proverbs 6:20-24 My son, keep your father's commandment, and forsake not your mother's teaching. Bind them on your heart always; tie them around your neck. When you walk, they will lead you; when you lie down, they will watch over you; and when you awake, they will talk with you. For the commandment is a lamp and the teaching a light, and the reproofs of discipline are the way of life, to preserve you from the evil woman, from the smooth tongue of the adulteress.

Proverbs 10:20 The tongue of the righteous is choice silver; the heart of the wicked is of little worth.

Proverbs 10:31 The mouth of the righteous brings forth wisdom, but the perverse tongue will be cut off.

Proverbs 12:18 There is one whose rash words are like sword thrusts, but the tongue of the wise brings healing.

Proverbs 12:19 Truthful lips endure forever, but a lying tongue is but for a moment.

Proverbs 15:2 The tongue of the wise commends knowledge, but the mouths of fools pour out folly.

Proverbs 16:1 The plans of the heart belong to man, but the answer of the tongue is from the LORD.

Proverbs 16:23 The heart of the wise makes his speech judicious and adds persuasiveness to his lips.

Proverbs 17:4 An evildoer listens to wicked lips, and a liar gives ear to a mischievous tongue.

Proverbs 17:20 A man of crooked heart does not discover good, and one with a dishonest tongue falls into calamity.

Proverbs 21:6 The getting of treasures by a lying tongue is a fleeting vapor and a snare of death.

Proverbs 25:23 The north wind brings forth rain, and a backbiting tongue, angry looks.

Proverbs 26:28 A lying tongue hates its victims, and a flattering mouth works ruin.

Proverbs 22:11 He who loves purity of heart, and whose speech is gracious, will have the king as his friend.

Proverbs 24:1-2 Be not envious of evil men, nor desire to be with them, for their hearts devise violence, and their lips talk of trouble.

Proverbs 25:15 With patience a ruler may be persuaded,and a soft tongue will break a bone.

Proverbs 28:23 Whoever rebukes a man will afterward find more favor than he who flatters with his tongue.

More Building Faith Family Resources

ABOUT THE AUTHOR

Steve Demme and his wife Sandra have been married since 1979. They have been blessed with four sons, three lovely daughters-in-law, and three special grandchildren.

Steve has served in full or part time pastoral ministry for many years after graduating from Gordon-Conwell Theological Seminary. He is the creator of Math-U-See and the founder of Building Faith Families and has served on the board of Joni and Friends, Eastern PA.

He produces a monthly newsletter, weekly podcasts, and regular posts https://www.facebook.com/stevedemme/

Steve is a regular speaker at home education conferences, men's ministry events, and family retreats. His desire is to strengthen, teach, encourage, validate, and exhort parents and families to follow the biblical model for the Christian home.

BUILDING FAITH FAMILIES

Exists to teach and encourage families to embrace the biblical model for the Christian home.

Scripture declares God created the sacred institution of the family. In His wisdom, He designed marriage to be between one man and one woman. We believe healthy God-fearing families are the basic building block for the church and society.

The family is foundational and transformational. Parents and children become more like Jesus as they lay their lives down for each other, pray for each other, and learn to love each other as God has loved them.

RESOURCES TO ENCOURAGE AND STRENGTHEN YOUR FAMILY

- The **Monthly Newsletter** is an encouraging exhortation as well as updates on Bible contests and upcoming speaking engagements.

- **Podcast** Each week an episode is released on our website, Itunes, and our Facebook page. These may be downloaded for free.

- **Seminars for free download** For over 20 years Steve has been speaking and teaching at conferences around the world. Many of his messages are available for your edification.

- **Regular Posts on Facebook** Like us and receive short uplifting insights from scripture or a biblical exhortation.

www.buildingfaithfamilies.org

CRISIS TO CHRIST,

THE HARDEST AND BEST YEAR OF MY LIFE

I have wounds, scars, baggage, and stuff from my past, which I have tried to ignore, but which is always present. In 2012 I was confronted with the distressing knowledge that my own wounds, which I thought were hidden and of no consequence, were wounding those closest to me, my wife and sons. I discovered I cannot hide my toxic issues for eventually they will leak out and hurt those who are closest to me, primarily my wife and children.

This difficult time, the hardest and best year of my life, was instrumental in changing my life and transforming my relationship with God and my family. On this journey I experienced pain which led me to acknowledge my own hurts and get help from the body of Christ to understand root causes of my distress and confront unbiblical thinking.

While I experienced incredible pain, I also discovered that my Heavenly Dad likes me just the way I am. Even though my path went through deep waters, God was with me every step of the way.

My motivation in writing is to affirm others who are going through similar valleys and tribulations. These hard journeys are normal for the Christian. Every person of note in scripture endured at least one life changing crisis. God uses these difficult times to work deep in our hearts, reveal more of Himself, and transform us into the image of His Son.

KNOWING GOD'S LOVE,

BECOMING ROOTED AND GROUNDED IN GRACE

Comprehending God's unconditional love is the cornerstone for the overarching commands to love God and our neighbor. For we are unable to love until we have first been loved. "We love, because He first loved us." (1 John 4:19) and "In this is love, not that we have loved God but that he loved us." (1 John 4:10)

The first, or as Jesus called it, the Great Command, is to love God. I began asking God to help me love Him with all my heart, soul, mind, and strength and was wonderfully surprised by how he answered my request.

Instead of awaking one morning with a burning love for God, which I expected, He began to steadily reveal how much He loved me. In 2012 I found myself believing in a new way that God knows me thoroughly and loves me completely. This knowledge that God likes me for who I am, and not based on what I do, has transformed my life.

As I have become more rooted and grounded in grace, my relationship with God is now much richer and deeper. My wife and I are closer than we have ever been. Knowing I am loved and accepted just as I am, has freed me to be more transparent and real as I relate with my sons and others.

TRANSFORMED IN LOVE,

LOVING OTHERS AS JESUS HAS LOVED US

John 15:9 revealed God not only loved the world, He loved me. Jesus says to His disciples, "As the Father has loved me, so have I loved you. Abide in my love." Just as the Father loved His Son, Jesus loves me the same way.

The secret to abiding in God's love is found in the next few verses. "If you keep my commandments, you will abide in my love, just as I have kept my Father's commandments and abide in His love. This is my commandment, that you love one another as I have loved you." (John 15:10, 12)

As I love others, as I have been loved, I will abide in the love of God. As a husband and father, my primary responsibilities are to love God, my wife, and my sons. I am writing as a man and sharing how God has led me to begin applying these principles in our home. But these principles are applicable to every believer.

The fruit of loving others as we have been loved will not only bless each of our homes, but our communities as well. "By this all people will know that you are my disciples, if you have love for one another." (John 13:34)

As family members pray for one another, bear each other's burdens, lay their lives down for each other, and learn to love one another as Jesus has loved them, they are transformed and become more like Jesus.

SPEAKING THE TRUTH IN LOVE,

LESSONS I'VE LEARNED ABOUT FAMILY COMMUNICATION

Most of what I've learned about communication, I acquired in the past few years during transitioning my business to a family owned business. The ability to communicate about difficult topics like business, values, your occupation, and a family's legacy takes effort and training.

As a husband and father, I have the potential to build up and encourage my family like no one else. I also have the ability to tear down and discourage my wife and sons. The Bible teaches effective principles of communication which are timeless.

My relationship with my wife and children has been transformed through godly safe communication. As I continue to grow in grace and the knowledge of God, I am in a better place to have open, transparent, and honest communication. While the skills we have acquired in being a clear speaker and an engaged listener are beneficial, investing time to have a quiet heart is essential. For out of the abundance of the heart, the mouth speaks.

I hope the principles we have learned and applied to such benefit in our own home and business will be a help to you on your journey. May the words of our mouth and the meditation of our heart be acceptable in your sight, O LORD, our Rock and our Redeemer. (from Psalms 19:14)

THE CHRISTIAN HOME AND FAMILY WORSHIP

In this readable and encouraging book, Steve shares practical scripture-based tips for teaching the word of God to children of all ages.

He also addresses common obstacles we all face in establishing the discipline of regular family worship.

Be encouraged by Steve's experiences teaching his four sons, and learn from other families who share strategies that have worked for their children. You may purchase this book, or participate in our Family Worship Challenge.

When you read or listen to *"The Christian Home and Family Worship"* within 30 days of receiving your copy, it is yours for FREE. If you are unable to fulfill this obligation, you agree to send a check for $50.00 to Building Faith Families. Steve will follow up with you at the end of thirty days. Contact Steve at sdemme@demmelearning.com

"I loved the book and read it in about a week and a half. My chief take-away was family worship needs to be an important part of family life. I've had five family worship times and I can definitely say I've already seen some fruits from these sessions. Your book had some great examples of how to make it more appealing to the kids."

"I was indeed able to read the book in time. The main thing I took away from it was the Nike slogan: "Just do it." So I did.

THE HYMNS FOR FAMILY WORSHIP

This time-honored collection of 62 classic hymns will be a rich addition to yourfamily worship. Make a joyful noise to the LORD!

In addition to the music for these carefully selected songs of worship, the history and origin of each hymn enhances the meaning of the lyrics.

There are three CDs with piano accompaniment for singing along in your home, car, or church.

Some of the titles are:

- A Mighty Fortress
- What a Friend We Have in Jesus
- Holy, Holy, Holy
- It Is Well With My Soul
- To God Be The Glory
- All Hail the Power of Jesus Name
- Amazing Grace
- How Firm a Foundation
- Blessed Assurance
- Christ Arose
- Rise Up O Men of God
- Just As I Am

Along with 50 more!

STEWARDSHIP

Stewardship is a biblical approach to personal finance. It is appropriate for anyone with a good grasp of basic math and has completed Algebra 1. I wrote this curriculum for a 15-16 year old student who was thinking about getting a job, purchasing a car, acquiring a credit card, and opening a bank account. It is full of practical application and the principles being taught are from a Christian Worldview. Many parents have commented they wish they had this class when they were a young adult.

Consider Stewardship for individual study, small group discussion, and adult ministries.

Stewardship Instruction Pack
The Stewardship Instruction Pack contains the instruction manual with lesson-by-lesson instructions, detailed solutions, Biblical Foundation, and the DVD with lesson-by-lesson video instruction.

Biblical Foundation
This concise 150 page book has thirty chapters that address a variety of topics for those who would be a faithful steward of God's resources. Steve references over 200 verses from Genesis to Revelation in sharing how God has helped him to apply scripture principles in his home and business. It is included in the Instruction Pack.

STEWARDSHIP

Stewardship Student Pack

The Stewardship Student Pack contains the Student Workbook with lesson-by-lesson worksheets, and review pages. It also includes the Stewardship Tests.

- Earning Money
- Percent
- Taxes
- Banking
- Checking
- Interest
- Investing
- Budgeting
- Percents at the Store
- Credit Cards
- Comparison Shopping
- Purchasing an Automobile
- Costs for Operating an Automobile
- Cost for Owning a Home versus Renting
- Making Change, and more

Thanks for this curriculum! This was the best math course I've taken in all my high school years, and I don't even like math :)

- Caleb

That your curriculum is Christ-centered has made the biggest difference in my homeschool experience.

- Sarah

My family and I just finished the Stewardship course. Thank you for another great Math-U-See program.

- Toby

Made in the USA
Middletown, DE
15 April 2016